THE PEOPLE'S DOONESBURY

DOONESBURY BOOKS BY G.B. TRUDEAU

Still a Few Bugs in the System
The President Is a Lot Smarter Than You Think
But This War Had Such Promise
Call Me When You Find America
Guilty, Guilty, Guilty!
"What Do We Have for the Witnesses, Johnnie?"
Dare To Be Great, Ms. Caucus
Wouldn't a Gremlin Have Been More Sensible?
"Speaking of Inalienable Rights, Amy..."
You're Never Too Old for Nuts and Berries
An Especially Tricky People
As the Kid Goes for Broke
Stalking the Perfect Tan
"Any Grooming Hints for Your Fans, Rollie?"
But the Pension Fund Was Just Sitting There
We're Not Out of the Woods Yet
A Tad Overweight, but Violet Eyes to Die For
And That's My Final Offer!
He's Never Heard of You, Either
In Search of Reagan's Brain

IN LARGE FORMAT

The Doonesbury Chronicles
Doonesbury's Greatest Hits
The People's Doonesbury

G.B.TRUDEAU

THE PEOPLE'S
DOONESBURY

NOTES FROM UNDERFOOT, 1978–1980

HOLT, RINEHART AND WINSTON · NEW YORK

Library of Congress Catalog Card Number: 81-80815
ISBN Hardbound: 0-03-049166-5
ISBN Paperback: 0-03-049171-1

Designer: Amy Hill
Printed in the United States of America

The cartoons in this book have appeared in newspapers
in the United States and abroad under the auspices of
Universal Press Syndicate.

1 3 5 7 9 10 8 6 4 2

TO THE MEMORY OF MY FRIEND
AND EDITOR, JIM ANDREWS

AN ANNOTATED CONVERSATION WITH THE AUTHOR

Publisher's Note: For the past several years, the editors of this imprint have sought to persuade cartoonist G. B. Trudeau to go on the record with some thoughts about his life and work. For a few exhilarating weeks before this volume went to press, Trudeau was believed to have been interested. His interest, however, did not blossom into actual consent, so the following interview was regrettably obtained under the false understanding it would only be published in a French film magazine.

   As rich in detail as the final transcript was, certain of the artist's references cried out for clarification or addenda, and, for this reason, his remarks have been periodically annotated.

Q: Given all the opportunities you've had, why have you resisted fame these many years?

A: I'm not altogether sure. Perhaps because it requires getting out more than I'd like. If you're serious about it, nurturing a public image, unlike building a reputation, is not something you can do in the privacy of your own living room. It's not just that fame is corrupting; it's time-consuming.[1] You're always busy trying to live up to your latest version of yourself.

Q: Aren't we all?

A: Yes, but it's nice not to have to shave beforehand. Listen, some years ago I did a talk show in Boston. I was twenty-two and I'd been doing the strip for about six months. After a brief introduction, the hostess turned to me and asked what it was like to be rich, famous, and eligible. I hadn't the faintest idea what she was talking about. After staring at her in dumb panic for about five seconds, I finally just rolled my eyes. The hostess looked very pleased and cut to a commercial. I never did another television show.[2]

Q: You must have been tempted, though. I read somewhere that you and Pope John Paul are the only two people ever to have turned down an interview with "60 Minutes."

A: Well, I don't think too much should be made of that. With the Pope, there was a scheduling conflict. They tried to book him on Easter, which is pretty arrogant if you think about it. In my case, I missed the message on my answering service.[3] Unless you've been defrauding widows out of their life savings, "60 Minutes" doesn't call twice.

[1] For Trudeau, so is anonymity. He once hid in his bathroom for three hours to avoid a reporter from the *Baltimore Sun*.

[2] Not entirely true. He did appear on "To Tell the Truth," where only one of the four panelists chose him over the two impostors. Trudeau walked away with $167 and a pair of jade cufflinks.

[3] Trudeau's answering service, VIP of New Haven, played a continuing role in the cartoonist's isolation from the outside world—at least it did until a crate of original strips belonging to Trudeau was removed from its office only to be recovered in a police raid on the Sunshine Girls Escort Service in Hamden, Connecticut. Sunshine's unlucky social director was subsequently convicted of first-degree larceny, partly on the strength of Trudeau's ability to recognize his own work in court.

Q: That sounds a shade ingenuous, but let's go on.... You are reported to go to some lengths when you are preparing a sequence in the strip. How much research do you really do?

A: As little as I can possibly get away with. It is for this quality above all others, I think, that I am so admired by undergraduates; I know just enough to create the impression I know a lot. And, of course, being a cartoonist helps. If it weren't for the hopelessly low expectations with which people turn to my section of the newspaper, I'm sure I would have been exposed years ago.

Q: You know, if you're going to continue being self-effacing, we might as well forget the whole thing. Frankly, it's not very interesting. Don't you feel good about yourself?

A: Of course I feel good about myself. You don't think I've got reason to? What's the Pulitzer Prize, chopped liver?[4]

Q: Okay, okay. Tell us about the prize.

A: What's to tell.... It's the classiest award in America. No dinner, no acceptance speeches, no TV show. They just call you up and say, "Good going, the check is in the mail." Everybody in my neighborhood was very proud of me. My grocer asked me what I was going to do with the two hundred thousand dollars. I think he thought I won the Pulitzer on a quiz show.[5]

Q: Speaking of easy money, why haven't you gotten into product licensing? The annual gross of the *Peanuts* empire is said to exceed the GNP of your average emerging nation.

A: Well, Sparky Schulz simply takes the position that the spin-offs make people happy. I have no problem with that position, but with the exception of the books, I prefer to keep my characters on the reservation. Perhaps it's because there's no logical connection between my characters and a lunch box... unless, of course, you find the logic of the profit motive irresistible.

Q: May we assume you'd loan your characters out for charity?[6]

A: You're missing the point. It's a matter of artistic pride. I think the case against merchandising was best made by the nine-year-old boy who once wrote to inquire why I wasn't selling any *Doonesbury* "by-products."

Q: You seem to be preoccupied with the idea of purity in your work.

[4]When Trudeau, in 1975, became the first comic-strip artist to win the Pulitzer Prize for Editorial Cartooning, the Editorial Cartoonists' Society proposed a resolution condemning the Pulitzer committee. Trudeau, once assured the award was irrevocable, supported the resolution.

[5]The award was actually in the amount of $2,000. Trudeau blew most of it on household bills and some unnecessary minor surgery.

[6]The interviewer's facetiousness was unwarranted. Trudeau had in fact once used several of his characters to promote a Connecticut Red Cross blood drive.

A: Somebody has to be. If you have a good editor, as I had for ten years in Jim Andrews, you come to realize that the inner life of a comic strip is a very fragile ecosystem.[7] It has its own rules, its own time frames, its own internal logic. That logic may be completely askew, but if you tinker with it, the chances are pretty good the whole thing will collapse.

Q: Could you elaborate?

A: Yes, but I'd rather not. I only put in that last bit for people who might be working on dissertations.

Q: That's very thoughtful, but...

A: Look, E. B. White once compared the analysis of humor to dissecting a frog; that is, it can be done, but the frog tends to die in the process.

Q: Where do you see satire going in the decade ahead?

A: You're asking me to predict a trend? You must be mad. I only do postmortems.

Q: All right, where has satire been? What about "Saturday Night Live"?

A: A magnificent missed opportunity. The reason why "SNL" ultimately doesn't matter is that the show never developed a point of view. Originally, the program produced some pretty good guerrilla theater, but with its success, it quickly evolved into a smug exercise in slash-and-burn humor—anarchy for its own sake. Nothing of value was ever left standing. This was a major failing, I think, because great satire has always had some sort of moral underpinnings—just ask Richard Pryor or Lily Tomlin.

Q: Or Garry Trudeau?

A: Yes, but don't look for conviction. I'm like Don Corleone. I've got a business to run.

Q: That's how you justify cuffing people for a living?

A: Absolutely. It's my job. I'm a form of social control. I make no apologies.

Q: Perhaps you should. One of the things that troubles some people about *Doonesbury* is that it's hard to know when you're reporting and when you're making things up. For instance, did Jerry Brown really solicit a political contribution from Sidney Korshak, the alleged organized-crime figure, as you charged in one series?

[7]Andrews realized Trudeau's limitations. He once described the cartoonist as "a thoughtful, creative, and highly concerned young man who is out to make a fast buck."

[8]When asked by NBC reporter Brian Ross, who originally broke the story, why he had solicited a contribution from a man chronically under federal investigation, Brown replied, "Even Jane Fonda was once investigated by the FBI." Later, he described other charges made in the strip as "false and libelous," but declined to press the issue on the novel grounds that "the First Amendment allows libel by the press."

[9]Tom Hayden, among other disinterested observers, wrote that Trudeau's view of Brown was "bigoted."

A: Yes. Actually, Brown doesn't deny this.[8] But most California papers killed the strips on the grounds that I had trampled the rights of a man the FBI had called one of the most influential mobsters in the country. Whimsically enough, the only two papers outside of Brown's home state to share this concern were located in — you guessed it — Reno and Las Vegas.

Q: Do you know Brown personally?

A: Nope. I once met Linda, which, of course, I recognize as not being the same thing.

Q: Some of Brown's admirers charge you've been uncommonly tough on him.[9] Perhaps if you got to know him, you'd feel differently about him.

A: Exactly. Which is as good an excuse as any to pass. One of the reasons why public figures get to be public figures in the first place is that they are not without charm. Insisting, as a George Will does, that one must get in close to make those lovely, nuanced judgment calls is utter nonsense. I'm not interested in private assurances or endearments, the insider's "access." I'm interested in what the outsider sees — the public face the politician *chooses* to project, *chooses* to be judged on. Nothing could be fairer. He's setting the agenda; I'm merely reacting.

Q: You're all heart.

A: Actually, I'm all boy. If you think this business is fun, you're right....

THE ROTUNDA STRIKES BACK

Q: Is it true that Tip O'Neill tried to head off a couple of strips about him during the Korean scandal?

A: Yes, but I think he was getting bad advice. A comic strip is not one of those things you want to look too worried about. One of the strips concerned a dubious nursing-home deal the speaker had drifted into.[1] To the delight of all the papers who picked up the story, this time I actually had my facts straight.[2] The other strip was a mail-in coupon, in which it was implied that Tip was among those who had benefited from Tongsun Park's largesse. It was a shameless gimmick, of course. And since the coupon was then reprinted in all the news stories, readers were given two opportunities to cut it out and send it in.

Q: How many did O'Neill receive?

A: Nobody knows. After the tenth bag of postcards was carted over to the Speaker's office, the post office was alerted to stop delivery. Now *that's* lobbying. It was a gun nut's wet dream.

[1] Gary Hymel, the Speaker's press secretary, offered to show Trudeau cancelled checks that he claimed absolved O'Neill from any impropriety. The offer was quickly withdrawn when Trudeau suggested that their authenticity be verified by *The New York Times.*

[2] And the courage to stand behind them. The artist's long-time mentor and confidant, Nicholas von Hoffman, later commended Trudeau for having the right stuff, saying that he had upheld the highest traditions of "investigative cartooning."

MAY I HAVE YOUR ATTENTION, PLEASE?

THROUGH AN UNFORTUNATE SET OF CIRCUMSTANCES, OUR SPEAKER TONIGHT, FORMER AMBASSADOR DUKE, HAS BEEN DELAYED!

IF YOU'LL ALL JUST BEAR WITH US, I'M SURE MR. DUKE WILL BE ARRIVING HERE JUST AS SOON AS HE IS ABLE!

OKAY, HOW MANY FINGERS? NINE.

..AND NOW, WITHOUT FURTHER ADO, THE PRINCE OF GONZO — AMBASSADOR *DUKE!*

YEAA! CLAP! CLAP! CLAP!

HE LOOKS A LITTLE SHAKY STILL, ZONKER.. THAT'S NORMAL. I JUST HOPE HE'S REASONABLY COHERENT!

GOOD EVENING. FEW OF NATURE'S WONDERS HAVE BEEN MORE WIDELY MISUNDERSTOOD THAN THE PLAYFUL PEYOTE BUTTON.

I THINK HE'S GOING TO BE OKAY.. MAY I HAVE THE FIRST SLIDE, PLEASE?

MR. DUKE, I'M THINKING OF BECOMING A REPORTER. WHAT ADVICE WOULD YOU GIVE SOMEONE WHO IS JUST STARTING OUT?

LOOK, JUNIOR, JOURNALISM IS A JUNGLE! NEVER FORGET THAT! IN JOURNALISM, THERE ARE NO WINNERS, JUST SURVIVORS! WE ARE TALKING SNAKE PIT *CITY*, SLIM!

SO DIG IT! I BEEN THERE! IF YOU FALTER FOR A *SECOND*, YOUR COLLEAGUES WILL *WASTE* YOU, WILL *SAVAGE* YOUR REP, YOUR NAME, YOUR.. YOUR..

WHAT WAS THE QUESTION AGAIN? UM.. HOW DO YOU LIKE OUR CAMPUS?

ANY FURTHER QUERIES? YES, MR. AMBASSADOR, WE MEMBERS OF THE AUDIENCE COULDN'T HELP NOTICING THAT YOU'RE STONED TO THE GILLS!

CONSIDERING YOUR SIZABLE LECTURE FEE, PAID IN PART BY CLASS DUES, CAN YOU THINK OF ANY REASON WHY WE SHOULDN'T BE GROSSLY INSULTED?

PSST! DUKE! YOUR MOM! LOOK, I WAS HOPING TO AVOID THE SUBJECT OF MOTHER'S TUMOR, BUT..

PROFESSOR KISSINGER, OL' WEINBURGER HERE'S BEEN MAKING A PRETTY STRONG CASE AGAINST GOING TO THE SHA-NA-NA'S DINNER! WHAT'S YOUR REPLY?

HEY, BARNEY..

NO, NO, IT'S ONLY FAIR! LET HIM GIVE HIS SIDE!

THANK YOU, MR. PERKINS. I'M GRATEFUL TO FINALLY HAVE A CHANCE TO PUT THE DINNER AND ITS SPONSOR IN THE PROP- ER PERSPECTIVE..

SPONSOR?

THE FRIENDS OF EXXON SOCIETY WAS FOUNDED IN..

NEVER MIND.

GOOD EVENING. THIS IS THE SCENE IN NEW YORK TONIGHT AS HUNDREDS OF DEMONSTRATORS GATHER OUT- SIDE A DINNER FOR THE EMPRESS OF IRAN. ROLAND HEDLEY IS THERE.

HARRY, THERE'S BEEN A SLIGHT DELAY IN THE FESTIVITIES TONIGHT AS WE AWAIT THE LATE ARRIVAL OF PRO-SHAH FORCES HERE AT THE NEW YORK HILTON HOTEL.

BAD WEATHER APPARENTLY DELAYED THE BUSES BRINGING THE SHAH'S RE- CRUITS TO N.Y., SO OUT OF FAIRNESS, PLANNERS HAVE HELD UP THE BANQUET TO ALLOW COUNTER DEMONSTRATORS TIME TO TAKE UP THEIR POSITIONS!

LONG LIVE THE SHAH!

..AND HERE THEY COME NOW! LOOKS LIKE THE EVENING'S UNDER WAY, HARRY!

HARRY, I'M TALKING TO A COUPLE OF STUDENTS RIGHT NOW, BUT UN- LIKE MOST OF THE FOREIGN DEMON- STRATORS HERE, THESE YOUNG MEN ARE AS AMERICAN AS YOU OR I!

MOREOVER, I AM TOLD THAT THEY ARE STUDENTS OF DR. HENRY KISSINGER, THE FEATURED SPEAK- ER AT TONIGHT'S DINNER HON- ORING THE EMPRESS!

GENTLEMEN, TELL ME, WHY ON EARTH ARE YOU WEARING THOSE MASKS? SURELY YOU'RE NOT PROTECTING RELATIVES OR LOVED ONES IN IRAN?

NO, BUT WE'VE GOT MIDTERMS COMING UP, MAN..

WHOA! SAY NO MORE!

HEY, LOOK! IT'S SHIRLEY MACLAINE!

SHIRLEY MACLAINE? I DON'T BELIEVE IT! WHAT'S SHE DOING HERE?

HEY, SHIRL! WHAT GIVES? DON'T YOU KNOW WHAT HAPPENS TO POLITICAL DISSIDENTS IN IRAN?

FOR YOUR INFORMATION, FELLAH, IRANIAN DISSIDENTS ARE SENT TO THE SHAH'S PRISONS, WHERE THEY ARE INTERROGATED, BRUTALIZED, AND RARELY HEARD FROM AGAIN!

OH. YOU HEARD, THEN.

THAT'S RIGHT. SO YOU CAN STOP ACTING SO DAMN SUPERIOR!

WITH THE SERVING OF A PÂTÉ DE FOIE GRAS AND A LIGHT CHABLIS, THE FRIENDS OF EXXON SOCIETY DINNER HONORING THE SHAHBANOU FARAH IS FINALLY UNDER WAY, HARRY..

DESPITE THE UGLY PROTESTS OUTSIDE, SOME OF OUR BRIGHTEST STARS HAVE TURNED OUT, RANGING FROM VACATIONING NEWSMAN WALTER CRONKITE TO TONIGHT'S BIGGEST SURPRISE, ACTIVIST SHIRLEY MacLAINE!

THE SHAH IS A *MURDERER!* THE SHAH IS A *MURDERER!!*

THE SHAH IS..AWK!

WELL, THE SPEECHES HAVE ALREADY BEGUN HERE AT THE HILTON BALLROOM, HARRY..

THE SHAH IS A MURDERER!

HARRY, THE SITUATION HERE ON THE BALLROOM FLOOR IS BEGINNING TO HEAT UP, TO SAY THE LEAST.

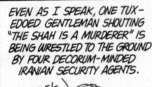
EVEN AS I SPEAK, ONE TUX-EDOED GENTLEMAN SHOUTING "THE SHAH IS A MURDERER" IS BEING WRESTLED TO THE GROUND BY FOUR DECORUM-MINDED IRANIAN SECURITY AGENTS.

>SCUFFLE!< =SCUFFLE!=

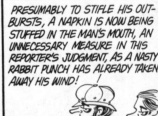
PRESUMABLY TO STIFLE HIS OUTBURSTS, A NAPKIN IS NOW BEING STUFFED IN THE MAN'S MOUTH, AN UNNECESSARY MEASURE IN THIS REPORTER'S JUDGMENT, AS A NASTY RABBIT PUNCH HAS ALREADY TAKEN AWAY HIS WIND!

DEMITASSE, SIR?

FOR THE EMPRESS'S REACTION, UP TO YOU AT THE HEAD TABLE, BARBARA!

>KNOCK! KNOCK!=

HEY, DIDN'T YOU *HEAR* ME? GO AWAY, DAMMIT, OR I'LL OPEN FIRE!

UNCLE DUKE! DON'T *SHOOT!* IT'S ME, ZONKER!

ZONKER! WHAT THE HELL ARE *YOU* DOING HERE?

I'M ON MIDTERM BREAK, UNCLE DUKE! DON'T YOU REMEMBER? YOU ASKED ME OUT HERE TO GO SKIING!

OH..OH.. RIGHT! OF COURSE, I DID! COME RIGHT ON IN, BOY!

AUNT SANDY'S AWAY, I SEE..

YEAH, SORRY ABOUT ALL THIS. MY PEACOCK'S BEEN SICK.

SO WHAT YOU BEEN UP TO, UNCLE DUKE? FOUND A NEW JOB YET?

NO, NOT YET..

BUT I'VE GOT ALL MY RESUMES OUT. I EXPECT I SHOULD BE HEARING SOMETHING PRETTY SOON...

WHAT SORT OF JOBS YOU APPLYING FOR?

OH, THE PRESIDENT OF YALE, HEAD OF ABC NEWS, MANAGER FOR THE REDSKINS, SOMETHING OF THIS NATURE...

SOMETHING OF WHAT NATURE?

YOU KNOW, SHOW BUSINESS. QUITE FRANKLY, NEPHEW, I'VE GOT THE BUG!

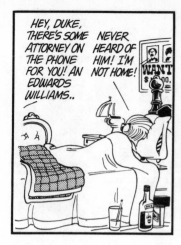

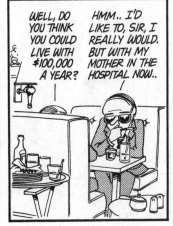

PEACOCK, I REPEAT: WE'VE LANDED LAGOS, REQUEST MINI-CAMS FOR J.C.'S MOTORCADE POOL!

ALSO, TELL NEW YORK WE'RE BOUNCING EVENING NEWS FEED OFF THE BIRD AT 5:30 EST!

ROGER, WILCO! OUT!

BZZ!.. BIP! CALLING STAR QUALITY! THIS IS VERTICAL HOLD! COME IN, STAR QUALITY!

"STAR QUALITY"?

GO AHEAD, VERTICAL HOLD! DO WE HAVE A ROGER FROM HAIR SPRAY?

WELL, SO MUCH FOR LAGOS! DID YOU CATCH MY STAND-UP TODAY, RICK?

NO, I'M AFRAID I MISSED IT, ROLAND. ANOTHER ELECTRIC PERFORMANCE?

WELL, IT WASN'T BAD! CAN'T BEAT THE IMMEDIACY OF TELEVISION, YOU KNOW, RICK?

YEAH! ESPECIALLY WITH A STORY LIKE CARTER'S LATEST OPEN-MIKE BLUNDER!

HIS WHAT?

WE'RE PLAYING IT PAGE ONE! IT HAS TO BE THE BIGGEST GAFFE HE'S EVER MADE, WOULDN'T YOU SAY?

UH.. YEAH! WHAT WERE HIS EXACT WORDS AGAIN?

I DUNNO, I JUST HOPE SADAT DOESN'T OVERREACT, YOU KNOW?

.. AND THEN THE CAMERA CUTS BACK TO ME ON A MEDIUM CLOSE-UP AS I SAY, "WAS THE CARTER JOURNEY A SUCCESS? ONLY TIME WILL TELL!"

HERE I DROP MY VOICE..."BUT IF THERE WAS ANYTHING OF SUBSTANCE TO BE DIVINED FROM THIS TRIP, IT COMPLETELY ESCAPED THE ATTENTION OF THIS REPORTER!"

THAT'S IT?

YUP. WHAT DO YOU THINK?

SURE YOU CAN AFFORD TO BE THAT HONEST?

HELL, YES! I CALL 'EM AS I SEE 'EM, RICK!

WELL, IT'S BEEN A PLEASURE RIDING WITH YOU, REDFERN! GIVE MY BEST TO EVERYONE AT THE "TIMES"!

TAP! TAP!

NBC News

THE "POST."

OH, RIGHT, THE WASHINGTON "POST." GOOD PAPER, THAT.

TAP! TAP!

NBC News

THANK YOU.

WHAT HAVE YOU PEOPLE BEEN UP TO SINCE YOU OVERTHREW THE GOVERNMENT, ANYWAY?

TAP! TAP!

NBC News

NOT SURE. SPORTS, I THINK.

BET YOU GUYS MISS THE HECK OUT OF THE TRICKSTER, HUH?

TAP! TAP!

NBC News

SO MUCH FOR MR. CARTER'S NOD TO THE THIRD WORLD! DID YOU KNOW HE'S ALREADY HOME?

WELL, OF COURSE, PHRED! HE HAS TO HOST THE ANNUAL HUMAN RIGHTS AWARDS BANQUET THIS WEEK!

OH, SAY, THAT'S RIGHT! YOU SENT IN YOUR NOMINATION FORM YET?

YOU BETTER BELIEVE IT! WITH ALL THIS NEW INTEREST IN AFRICA, BENIN FINALLY HAS A REAL CHANCE!

LOOK AT THE CURVE ON THIS CHART WE PREPARED! THE INCIDENCE OF CURTAILED LIBERTIES HAS DROPPED OFF SIGNIFICANTLY! AND CHECK OUT THESE BEFORE-AND-AFTER PHOTOS OF TYPICAL POLITICAL PRISONERS!

WOW! WHAT A DIFFERENCE!

COMPLETELY UNRETOUCHED! AND WE GOT AFFIDAVITS, TOO!

VICTOR, HOW'D THIS HUMAN RIGHTS AWARDS BANQUET GET STARTED ANYWAY?

WELL, AS I UNDERSTAND IT, IT'S THE BRAINCHILD OF THE U.S. SECRETARY OF SYMBOLISM.

EVERY YEAR, HE PRESENTS AWARDS TO THOSE NATIONS WHO SHOW THE MOST IMPROVEMENT IN FURTHERING PERSONAL LIBERTIES, AS CERTIFIED BY AMNESTY INTERNATIONAL!

HERE, TAKE A LOOK! IT'S ALL EXPLAINED IN THIS WHITE HOUSE BROCHURE OUTLINING THE AWARDS AND THEIR QUALIFICATIONS..

"THE JAMES EARL CARTER ATONEMENT CUP, GIVEN EACH YEAR TO.."

THAT'S THE MOST COVETED, OF COURSE.

WELL, SEE YOU AT THE HUMAN RIGHTS BANQUET, VICTOR!

OKAY, PHRED! I MIGHT BE A LITTLE LATE. I'VE GOT TO DO SOME LAST MINUTE LOBBYING..

THE COMPETITION'S THAT INTENSE, HUH?

ARE YOU KIDDING? BILLIONS IN U.S. AID CAN HANG ON THE OUTCOME! YOU CAN'T BELIEVE THE LENGTHS SOME COUNTRIES GO TO!

WHY, LAST YEAR, PRESIDENT MARCOS OF THE PHILIPPINES EVEN TRIED RESTORING DEMOCRACY A WEEK BEFORE THE DEADLINE! OF COURSE, IT DIDN'T WORK.

NO AWARD?

NO DEMOCRACY. TURNED OUT HIS PEOPLE WEREN'T READY FOR IT.

GOOD EVENING, FRIENDS, AND WELCOME TO THE SECOND ANNUAL HUMAN RIGHTS AWARDS BANQUET!

BEFORE WE GET STARTED, I'D JUST LIKE TO SAY THAT THESE AWARDS WOULDN'T BE POSSIBLE IF NOT FOR REPORTS FURNISHED US BY HUMAN RIGHTS WATCHDOG AMNESTY INTERNATIONAL!

BOOOO!! BOOO! HISSS!

AND WELL YOU MIGHT BOO!

HA! HA, HA! HA, HA! HA! HA!

GBTrudeau

BOY, THERE SURE ARE A LOT OF CATEGORIES..

YES, THEY'VE EXPANDED IT CONSIDERABLY FROM LAST YEAR.

IT'S A SHAME, REALLY. I THINK THEY'VE DEVALUED THE HUMAN RIGHTS AWARDS BY OFFERING SO MANY..

LADIES AND GENTLEMEN, MAY I HAVE YOUR ATTENTION, PLEASE? IN OUR FIRST CATEGORY..

HERE WE GO! NEED A PENCIL?

FOR MOST COURTEOUS CUSTOMS OFFICIALS..

TEN BUCKS ON BER-MUDA!

HMM.. THEY STILL USING PINK JEEPS?

FOR MOST IMPROVED HUMAN RIGHTS CLIMATE IN A DEVELOPING NATION..

WE'VE GOT IT! I JUST KNOW WE'VE GOT IT!

BENIN'S A CHANGED COUNTRY, PHRED! CIVIL LIBERTIES AND THEN SOME! LAST YEAR ALONE WE RELEASED OVER 50 POLITICAL PRISONERS!

..AND THE WINNER IS.. GUINEA!

WHAT?!

GEE, VICTOR, I'M REALLY SORRY..

THAT DOES IT! BACK IN THE SLAMMER!

.. AND THE WINNER OF MOST IMPROVED CLIMATE FOR PUBLIC DEBATE WITHIN AN AUTHORITARIAN POLITICAL REGIME IS.. NICARAGUA!

YEAAA! BRAVO! BRAVO! CLAP! CLAP! CLAP! CLAP! CLAP! CLAP!

THANK YOU VERY MUCH! I'D JUST LIKE TO SAY THAT THE REFORMS IN MY COUNTRY WERE A DIRECT RESULT OF PRESSURE FROM THE U.S.!

UNITED STATES PRESSURE! ISN'T THAT GREAT, LADIES AND GENTLEMEN?!

IF YOU GUYS HADN'T PUT THE SCREWS ON, WE'D STILL BE IN THE DARK AGES!

CLAP CLAP

..AND THE FINAL AWARD OF THE EVENING GOES TO THAT NATION WHOSE SENSE OF MISSION AND HIGH MORAL PURPOSE MOST CLOSELY RESEMBLES THAT OF THE UNITED STATES!

>RIP!< .. AND THE WINNER IS..

WHOA.. WHAT HAVE WE GOT HERE? IT LOOKS LIKE A NINE-WAY TIE!

IT'S.. WESTERN EUROPE!

ACCEPTING FOR THE WEST IS NATO'S ALEXANDER HAIG..

THIS IS MELLOW HOTLINE! WHERE'S YOUR HEAD AT?

IT'S IN A BAD PLACE, DAN. I'M INCREDIBLY BUMMED OUT!

WHAT WENT DOWN, SEE, IS THAT MY LOVER AND I HAD MY EX OVER FOR DINNER, AND, LIKE, WE GOT INTO THIS INCREDIBLE HIGH-ENERGY RAP ON WHALES Y'KNOW?

WELL, MY LOVER COULDN'T HANDLE THE TRIP, AND EVER SINCE, HE'S BEEN DOING A REAL ANXIETY NUMBER ON ME, AND LIKE, WE HAVEN'T BEEN ABLE TO RELATE TO EACH OTHER FOR WEEKS!

HMM..HAVE YOU TRIED JOGGING TOGETHER?

YEAH, BUT YOU KNOW SCORPIOS. COMMITMENT-WISE, THERE'S NO PERCENTAGE IN IT!

HELLO, THIS IS MELLOW HOTLINE! WHERE'S YOUR HEAD AT?

UM..YEAH, I'D JUST LIKE TO SAY, LIKE..UM, Y'KNOW, LIKE, Y'KNOW, I'M, LIKE, Y'KNOW, UM..Y'KNOW?

FOR SURE, MAN. I KNOW JUST WHERE YOU'RE COMING FROM.

YOU DO?

FOR SURE! YOU'RE HAVING A HEAD TRIP. YOU'RE IN THIS WEIRD SPACE.

OH, WOW.. YEAH, I CAN RELATE TO THAT! THANKS A LOT, DAN!

YOU SURE GIVE GOOD MELLOW, DAN.

HEY, I WROTE THE BOOK, DIDN'T I?

DUKE, THERE'S NO WAY WE'RE GONNA GET ANY OF THESE KIDS! THE BEST OF THEM WILL BE ALL GONE BY ROUND SEVEN.

SEVEN? WE CAN'T MAKE A PICK UNTIL ROUND SEVEN?

THAT'S RIGHT. OUR TOP DRAFT CHOICES HAVE BEEN LONG SINCE TRADED AWAY..

A POX ON GEORGE ALLEN! NO WONDER THE TALENTLESS TOAD BOLTED TOWN WHEN HE DID!

TELL ME ABOUT IT. THIS IS THE THIRD YEAR I'VE HAD TO JUNK MY SCOUTING REPORTS!

I JUST DON'T SEE HOW HE GOT AWAY WITH THAT "THE FUTURE IS NOW" GARBAGE AS LONG AS HE DID!

I GUESS BECAUSE NOBODY ELSE HERE UNDERSTOOD POETRY.

YEAH, WELL, THINGS ARE GOING TO CHANGE AROUND HERE!

WELL, DUKE, IF WE CAN'T DRAFT, WE MIGHT AS WELL GO SHOPPING. GOT ANY FREE AGENTS YOU LIKE?

YEAH, HOW ABOUT "LAVA-LAVA" LENNY? YOU FAMILIAR WITH "LAVA-LAVA'S" WORK?

NOPE. WHO IS HE?

A KID I DISCOVERED SLINGING COCONUTS DURING MY TENURE IN PAGO PAGO. HE'S NOW PLAYING FRONT FOUR FOR THE LIONS.

ALL FRONT FOUR? SOUNDS LIKE A BIG BOY..

BIG? BOBBY, THE OPPOSITION'S LUCKY IF IT EVEN GETS A GLIMPSE OF THE QUARTERBACK!

UH-HUH..

I'M NOT KIDDING! WHEN I FIRST SAW HIM IN SAMOA, I THOUGHT HE WAS AN OFFSHORE ISLAND!

SO TELL ME MORE ABOUT THIS "LAVA-LAVA" LENNY, DUKE..

WELL, TO BEGIN WITH, HE'S THE BIGGEST LINEMAN TO COME OUT OF THE PACIFIC IN TWENTY YEARS!

THEY'RE SO RESPECTFUL OF HIS TALENTS IN DETROIT THAT HE HAS HIS OWN HANDLER! THIS KID HAS TO BE SEEN TO BE BELIEVED!

ANY PERSONALITY QUIRKS?

NONE THAT I'M AWARE OF. UNLESS YOU WANT TO INCLUDE A VILE TEMPER.

OH? WHAT'S HE PLAY ON?

FRESH PINEAPPLE. THEY FEED HIM AFTER EVERY TACKLE.

WHAT IS IT, BEV?

MR. DUKE, "LAVA-LAVA" LENNY'S ATTORNEY IS ON THE LINE.

THANKS, BABE. PUT HIM ON.. HELLO, HOOK? IT'S DUKE!

HI, THERE, DUKE! YOU GET MY CONTRACT PROPOSAL YET?

YEAH, I WAS JUST GOING OVER IT, AND IT'S COMPLETELY OUT OF LINE! WHAT'S THIS ABOUT THE KID NEEDING HIS OWN UNIVERSAL GYM?

NO CHOICE ON THAT, DUKE. HE'S JUST TOO BIG FOR THE STANDARD MODELS.

OH, YEAH? WELL, HOW ABOUT HIS OWN MEAT LOCKER?

HE'S A GROWING BOY, DUKE! LOOK, YOU WANT A COMPETITOR OR NOT?

OKAY, HOOK, YOU'RE ROBBING ME BLIND, BUT I THINK WE CAN WORK SOMETHING OUT..

I'M GLAD TO HEAR IT, DUKE.

FRANKLY, THE 'SKINS NEED "LAVA-LAVA", AND I'LL BE WILLING TO MAKE YOU A FIRM OFFER ON MONDAY!

MONDAY? WHY NOT NOW?

I GOTTA CONFER WITH THE MONEY, HOOK. YOU UNDERSTAND. JUST A FORMALITY.

OKAY, MONDAY IT IS. I'LL PREPARE MY CLIENT.

THANKS, HOOK. YOU'RE A PRINCE.

I KNOW. HOW DO YOU WANT HIM SHIPPED?

THAT'S RIGHT, MIKE, IN THE EIGHTH AND NINTH ROUNDS, DRAFT THEM BOTH! WE'RE STILL WEAK IN THE MIDDLE!

THE HELL WE ARE!

HUH?

YOUR PRAYERS HAVE BEEN ANSWERED, BOBBY BOY! GUESS WHO JUST SIGNED WITH YOURS TRULY?

NOT "LAVA-LAVA"?

390 LBS. OF STEAMING SAMOAN! OUR FRONT FOUR PROBLEMS ARE OVER!

MIKE? CANCEL THAT ORDER OF BUCKEYES!

BARTENDER! CHAMPAGNE FOR EVERYONE ON MR. WILLIAMS!

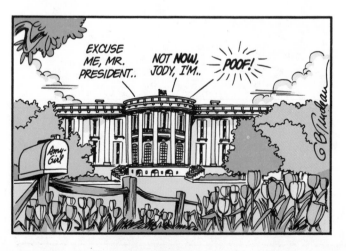

THIS IS ROLAND BURTON HEDLEY, JR.! AT ROCKE-FELLER CENTER TONIGHT, TENSIONS ARE MOUNTING AS THE NBC TELEVISION NETWORK AWAITS ITS NEW MESSIAH, FRED P. SILVERMAN.

CAN THE GENIUS BEHIND "THE LOVE BOAT" AND "CAPTAIN CAVEMAN AND THE TEENANGELS" RESTORE THE FORTUNES OF LAST-PLACE NBC? A RECENT DEVELOPMENT SUGGESTS HE MIGHT..

ABC WIDE WORLD OF NEWS HAS LEARNED THAT WHEN FREDDY SILVERMAN ARRIVES AT NBC THIS WEEK, HE WILL PROPOSE A POLICY OF PRIME-TIME *FRONTAL NUDITY!*

ALSO, CHIMPS. BUT WE'LL GET TO THAT LATER. FOR DETAILS ON THE NUDITY, LET'S GO TO CHICAGO..

CHICAGO?

YES, AS THE COUNT-DOWN CONTINUES, THE NAME OF THE GAME AT NBC IS "WAITING FOR FREDDY."

CAN SILVERMAN TURN THINGS AROUND FOR THE LOWLY NETWORK? WELL, IT'S ANYONE'S GUESS. IN THE RATINGS GAME THERE IS ONLY ONE QUESTION: HOW LOW ARE YOU WILL-ING TO SINK?

NO ONE, IT SEEMS, IS IMMUNE. EVEN THE NEW TAG-TEAM ANCHOR FORMAT RIGHT HERE AT ABC WIDE WORLD OF NEWS WAS A-DOPTED AS A DESPERATE, LAST-DITCH RESPONSE TO SAGGING RATINGS.

BACK TO YOU, FRANK, PETER, AND MAX. THANKS.

THANK YOU, ROLLIE.

YES, THANKS. IN OTHER NEWS..

THE LONG VIGIL IS OVER. EVEN AS I SPEAK, FRED P. SILVERMAN IS SPINNING HIS MILLION-DOLLAR WHEELS FOR THIRD-PLACE NBC!

ALREADY, THE NEW MAN HAS BEGUN TO LIVE UP TO HIS IMAGE AS A HARD WORKER. SILVERMAN IS SAID TO HAVE REPORTED TO WORK THIS MORNING AT 5:30 A.M.!

AND NOW, ADMIDST GROWING RU-MORS THAT THEIR NEW BOSS EVEN SKIPPED LUNCH, NBC EXECUTIVES ARE ANXIOUSLY AWAITING THE OUTCOME OF FREDDY'S PROGRAMING MAGIC!

ANY CHANGE YET?

YES..YES! BY GOD, HE'S TURNING IT AROUND!

LOOK OUT, WONDER CHIMP!

BLAM! BLAM!

FRED SILVERMAN. ON TOP. THE MAN OF THE MOMENT. BUT WHAT OF THE LOSERS? WHAT HAPPENS TO THEM? CORRESPONDENT ROLAND HEDLEY TALKED TO THE SEC-RETARY OF NBC'S DEPOSED HERB SCHLOSSER.

MISS JENKINS, WHAT WAS IT LIKE TO WORK FOR HERB SCHLOSSER?

WHO? I DON'T RECALL ANY-ONE BY THAT NAME.

COME NOW, MISS JENKINS, FOR THE LAST TWELVE YEARS YOU WERE HIS PER..

I DON'T *KNOW* HIM, I TELL YOU! LEAVE ME *ALONE!*

FOR MORE ON THE STORY, WE HAVE THIS RE-PORT FROM SIBERIA.

SPRING COMES LATE TO THE URAL MOUNTAINS..

"..AND I'M OUTRAGED," SAYS REP. LACEY DAVENPORT, "THAT THE COMMITTEE HAS REFUSED TO MOVE FORTHRIGHTLY ON THE KOREAN PAYOFF SCANDAL!"

ISN'T THAT INCREDIBLE, ZONKER? THIRTY CONGRESSMEN IMPLICATED, AND STILL NO HEARINGS OR DISCIPLINARY ACTION!

HMM.. MAYBE THEY'RE ALL INNOCENT.

IS IT TRUE YOU GREW UP NEAR DISNEYLAND, ZONKER?

YUP. I USED TO COMMUTE.

YOU KNOW, Z, I'D REALLY LIKE TO GET THE STORY ON THIS KOREAN SCAM. I WONDER IF I COULD GET LACEY DAVENPORT ON MY RADIO SHOW..

YOU KNOW HER?

UH-HUH. I MET HER AT REUNIONS WHILE BARTENDING A COUPLE YEARS AGO..

YEAH, I THINK I'LL GIVE HER A CALL. I'LL BET MY LISTENERS WOULD GIVE ANYTHING TO HEAR WHAT'S REALLY GOING ON IN THE HOUSE ETHICS COMMITTEE, YOU KNOW?

YOU KNOW?

WHILE YOU'RE AT IT, WHY DON'T YOU READ THEM THE PHONE BOOK?

WHAT'D LACEY SAY, MARK?

SHE AGREED TO DO THE INTERVIEW! I'M GOING TO FLY TO WASHINGTON TONIGHT!

WHAT? YOU'RE GOING ALL THE WAY DOWN THERE?

WELL, OF COURSE! FOR A LIVE REMOTE! I'LL JUST HOOK THE MIKE UP TO A PHONE, AND YOU CAN ANCHOR THE SHOW FROM BACK HERE.

ME? NOW, WAIT A MINUTE, MARK! THAT'S PUBLIC AFFAIRS! I CAN'T HANDLE A PUBLIC AFFAIRS SHOW, MAN!

SURE YOU CAN! WHY CAN'T YOU?

FOR CRYING OUT LOUD, MARK! I DON'T EVEN KNOW WHO'S PRESIDENT!

NEITHER DOES ANYONE ELSE. YOU'RE IN TUNE WITH THE TIMES.

I CERTAINLY APPRECIATE YOUR FINDING THE TIME TO TALK TO ME, MRS. D!

WELL, IT'S ALWAYS LOVELY TO SEE YOU, DEAR. I LOOK FORWARD TO OUR LITTLE CHAT..

HI, HO! WHO'S THIS?

DICK, YOU REMEMBER MARK SLACKMEYER, DON'T YOU? FROM THE CAMPUS RADIO STATION?

OH. SURE, I REMEMBER. GOOD TO SEE YOU AGAIN, SON!

THANK YOU, SIR.

I SUPPOSE YOU'RE HERE ABOUT THOSE DREARY LITTLE ORIENTALS.

UH..

IT'S BEEN A LONG WINTER, DEAR. WHY DON'T WE ALL SIT DOWN?

LACEY, FOR SOME TIME, YOUR COMMITTEE HAS BEEN WAITING TO HEAR THE TESTIMONY OF FORMER KOREAN AMBASSADOR KIM. DO YOU THINK KIM'S COOPERATION COULD GET THE INVESTIGATION BACK ON TRACK?

YES, BUT YOU SEE, DEAR, IT'S NOT REALLY THE INVESTIGATION THAT'S BEEN LAGGING. WHY, WE HAVE LOADS OF EVIDENCE!

WHAT IS LACKING IS THE COMMITTEE'S MOTIVATION TO ACT ON THE ALLEGATIONS. SINCE CONGRESS HAS NO INTENTION OF TAKING STRONG MEASURES, IT'S BECOME JUST A QUESTION OF HOW TO PUT ON THE BEST FACE.

A PUBLIC RELATIONS PROBLEM?

RIGHT. IN FACT, WE'RE ALL THINKING OF GOING TO CHINA.

MRS. DAVENPORT, I WONDER IF YOU COULD COMMENT ON THE LAVISH PARTIES THROWN BY KOREAN BUSINESSMAN PARK FOR HOUSE SPEAKER TIP O'NEILL.

WELL, DEAR, I WOULDN'T MAKE TOO MUCH OF THAT. YOU SEE, TIP'S A VERY POPULAR MAN, AND PEOPLE SIMPLY LIKE TO DO THINGS FOR HIM..

FOR INSTANCE, SOME BANKING PALS OF HIS ONCE OFFERED HIM A FREE INTEREST IN A NURSING HOME. RATHER THAN OFFEND HIS FRIENDS OVER A SILLY PRINCIPLE, HE GRACIOUSLY ACCEPTED.

JUST LETS PEOPLE WALK ALL OVER HIM, EH?

QUITE RIGHT. HE JUST DOESN'T SEEM TO KNOW HOW TO SAY NO!

WELL, LISTENERS, THERE YOU HAVE IT! PORTRAIT OF A COVER-UP! ARE YOU INCENSED BY IT? ARE YOU WONDERING WHAT YOU COULD DO TO MAKE LACEY'S JOB EASIER?

WELL, AS A PUBLIC SERVICE, WBBY RADIO HAS TAKEN OUT A COUPON AD IN YOUR LOCAL PAPER — JUST LIKE THE ONES THE GUN NUTS USE! SO IF YOU'RE MAD, CLIP THE COUPON! PASTE IT ON A POSTCARD, AND MAIL WITHOUT DELAY!

ACT NOW!

Congressman
Thomas O'Neill
House Speaker
U.S. Congress
Washington, D.C.
20515

Dear Tip:
Yes! I would like more information on the following: (Check one or more)
☐ Rep. C.E. Gallagher ($221,000)
☐ Rep. Edwin Edwards ($25,000)
☐ Rep. Wm. Minshall ($31,000)

☐ Rep. N. Galifianakis ($10,500)
☐ Rep. John J. McFall ($4,000)
☐ 25 Other Representatives ($?)
☐ 6 Senators ($?)
☐ Yourself ($6,000 in parties)
Hold public hearings now!
Yours for a Clean Congress,

Name _____
Address _____

WELL, MRS. D, I'D LIKE TO THANK YOU ONCE AGAIN FOR BEING TODAY'S "PROFILE ON PARADE."

WELL, IT WAS MY PLEASURE, MARK.

I'M SURE I SPEAK FOR ALL MY LISTENERS WHEN I WISH YOU THE BEST OF LUCK IN YOUR EFFORTS TO FLUSH THE BUMS OUT!

THANK YOU VERY MUCH.

WELL, THAT ABOUT WRAPS IT UP DOWN HERE IN THE NATION'S CAPITAL! BACK TO YOU, ZONKER!

UH.. ZONKER?

NOT SO FAST, FELLAH! I ORDERED ANCHOVIES, NOT SAUSAGE!

THE FALL OF MALIBU

Q: Tell us about Zonker's beach.

A: Well, technically, it's not really his beach. It's simply named after him. The Zonker Harris Memorial Beach. It was one of the private Malibu beaches recently liberated by the California Coastal Commission.[1] The residents were, of course, furious, and the redwood sign marking the access route was vandalized within twenty-four hours.

[1]Don Neuwirth, the project manager, told the *Los Angeles Times* that beach access in Malibu was a victory for the public. "If you take a picture of us erecting the sign," he said, "try to make it look like the raising of the flag at Iwo Jima."

ZONKER?.. IT'S ME, CORNELL. YOUR DAD CALLED ME WITH THE NEWS..

I'M REAL SORRY TO HEAR ABOUT THE TANNING CLINICS, ZONK, I REALLY AM.

THANKS, MAN, I APPRECIATE THAT..

WERE YOU GOING FOR IT THIS YEAR, Z? WERE YOU ON A HOT ROLL?

ARE YOU KIDDING? I WAS ONE SHADE AWAY FROM QUALIFYING FOR THE GEORGE HAMILTON COPPERTONE PRO-AM CELEBRITY COCOA BUTTER OPEN!

ARE YOU KIDDING? LET ME SEE..

IT DOESN'T SHOW NOW. I'M TOO UPSET..

I APPRECIATE YOUR DROPPING BY, OL' SCHOOLCHUM, BUT I'M AFRAID YOUR SYMPATHY CAN'T HELP ME NOW..

I COULD HAVE BEEN THE BEST, CORNELL. I COULD HAVE BEEN A CONTENDER. THE GEORGE HAMILTON COCOA BUTTER OPEN WAS WITHIN REACH. IT'S THE END OF A DREAM..

WHERE WILL YOU GO, ZONKER? WHAT WILL YOU DO WITH YOUR LIFE NOW?

I DUNNO, MAN, I JUST DUNNO. MAYBE DENTISTRY..

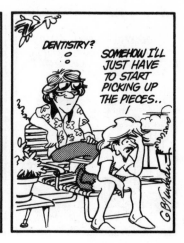

DENTISTRY?

SOMEHOW I'LL JUST HAVE TO START PICKING UP THE PIECES..

WHAT IS IT, KID?

I'VE GOT SOME PURCHASE ORDERS FOR YOU TO SIGN, MR. DUKE..

OH.. THANKS. WHO ARE YOU, ANYWAY?

RILEY, SIR. I'M YOUR NEW ASSISTANT.

ASSISTANT? I DIDN'T ASK FOR ANY ASSISTANT!

I WOULDN'T KNOW, SIR. I WAS JUST TOLD TO REPORT TO YOU.

YOU'RE A NARC, RIGHT, RILEY?

NO, SIR. THE OWNER'S NEPHEW. MAY I HAVE THE AFTERNOON OFF?

SIR, I UNDERSTAND YOU'RE DEVELOPING A NEW SPORTS MEDICINE PROGRAM..

THAT'S RIGHT, RILEY. THE WAY I SEE IT, THE REDSKINS DESERVE THE BEST.

WHEN A PLAYER GOES OUT ONTO THAT FIELD, I BELIEVE HE HAS EVERY RIGHT TO EXPECT CHEMICAL PARITY WITH THE OPPOSING TEAM!

WOW.. WHAT A RESPONSIBILITY!

YOU BETTER BELIEVE IT.

WHAT CAN I DO TO HELP, BOSS?

WELL, I SUPPOSE YOU COULD STAND LOOKOUT.

WOULD YOU HOLD ON, PLEASE, MR. DUKE?

I'D BE HAPPY TO.

HEY, WHAT GIVES, BOSS? YOU ALREADY HAVE A JOB..

RILEY, MY BOY, IT'S A ONCE IN A LIFE-TIME OPENING. I'D BE A FOOL NOT TO AT LEAST GIVE IT A SHOT.

BUT WHAT ABOUT YOUR CONTRACT WITH THE 'SKINS? YOU'RE COMMIT-TED TO A..

FOR GOD'S SAKE, BOY, I'M ONLY PUTTING OUT FEELERS! I HAVEN'T SAID I'M QUITTING YET..

AND HE'S AN EXPERT ON DRUG ABUSE?

YES, SIR. HE SAYS IT'S HIS LIFE.

MR. DUKE, YOU UNDERSTAND, OF COURSE, THAT AFTER THE BOURNE INCIDENT, THE PRESI-DENT IS ANXIOUS TO FIND A REPLACEMENT WITH IN-CONTESTABLE REPUTABILITY..

REPUTABILITY? MR. POWELL, WHEN IT COMES TO DISTINCTION IN THE FIELD OF DRUG ABUSE, I HAVE WHAT YOU MIGHT CALL AN EMBARRASS-MENT OF RICHES!

WHY, LEADING AUTHORITIES THE WORLD OVER CAN'T SAY ENOUGH ABOUT MY WORK! HERE, LET ME PUT ON MY COLLEAGUE, DR. P. Z. RILEY, DISTINGUISHED PRO-FESSOR EMERITUS OF ALKA-LOID DERIVATIVES..

WHO?

NOW, FOR GOD'S SAKE, DON'T LET YOUR VOICE CRACK, BOY!

YOU GOT THE JOB INTER-VIEW?

YOU BET I DID! I'M DUE AT THE WHITE HOUSE IN TWO HOURS!

I WISH I COULD DECIDE WHAT TO WEAR. I'D LIKE TO WEAR MY WEREWOLF COSTUME, BUT THE DAMN THING'S IN STORAGE FOR THE SUMMER!

UH..BOSS, YOU SURE YOU'RE UP TO AN IN-TERVIEW?

OF COURSE, I'M UP TO IT! WHY WOULDN'T I BE?

I DUNNO.. YOU JUST SEEM STRANGE TODAY..

I WOULDN'T GO POINTING FINGERS IF I WERE YOU, BOY!

BESIDES HIS WORK FOR THE GOVERNMENT, HE ALSO CLAIMS TO HAVE BEEN A LIFE-LONG ADVOCATE OF RESPON-SIBLE POLICY IN DRUG USE.

WELL, THAT WOULD BE A REFRESHING CHANGE FROM BOURNE. OKAY, LET'S CHECK HIM OUT..

MR. DUKE, WOULD YOU COME IN, PLEASE? ..UH.. MR. DUKE?

ERP!

MR. DUKE? ARE YOU OKAY?

OF COURSE, I AM! NICE PLACE YOU GOT HERE.

JOAN, I'VE BEEN LOOKING INTO YOUR REDRESS OPTIONS, DEAR..

AND?

WELL, THE PROBLEM IS THAT YOU'RE BEING DENIED FAIR SALARY AS A HOUSE EMPLOYEE WORKING FOR THE ETHICS COMMITTEE..

THIS I KNOW.

YES, BUT WHAT YOU PROBABLY DON'T KNOW IS WHO ARBITRATES SUCH COMPLAINTS!

YOU'RE ABOUT TO TELL ME THAT IT'S THE ETHICS COMMITTEE.

AT LEAST YOU'VE MET EVERYONE.

YEAH, BUT IT TOOK TWO YEARS.

THIS CERTAINLY IS A KNOTTY PROBLEM FOR YOU, DEAR. THE PRECEDENTS FOR YOUR CASE ARE SO SCANTY..

YOU KNOW WHAT I'D DO IF I WERE YOU, DEAR? I'D CALL UP A TOP LAW FIRM AND PUT A FULL COMPLEMENT OF ATTORNEYS ON RESEARCH! THEN I'D HIRE A TEAM OF..

LACEY..

NO.. NO, WAIT A MINUTE. THAT WOULDN'T WORK FOR YOU, WOULD IT?

I'M AFRAID NOT.

I KEEP FORGETTING YOU'RE NOT INDEPENDENTLY WEALTHY.

SO DOES MY BUTCHER.

YES, THIS IS MRS. DAVENPORT.

MA'AM, I'M CALLING FROM ACCOUNTING WITH THE INFORMATION YOU REQUESTED..

YOUR HUNCH ABOUT THAT YOUNG LAWYER WAS RIGHT. HIS SALARY WAS INCORRECTLY PROGRAMMED IN THE COMPUTER. WE'VE READJUSTED IT DOWN TO HIS PROPER SCALE. I HOPE HE WON'T BE TOO INCONVENIENCED..

NO, NO, I'M SURE NOT. YOU CAUGHT IT EARLY. THANKS VERY MUCH..

OF COURSE, ANY KIND OF CONDO IS A TERRIFIC INVESTMENT THESE DAYS!

I'M SURE YOU MADE THE RIGHT DECISION, WOODY.

I SUPPOSE YOU HEARD THE COMPUTER PICKED UP THE DISCREPANCY IN OUR SALARIES..

YES, I DID, WOODY. LACEY JUST CALLED. I HOPE YOU DON'T BLAME ME..!

NO, NO, IT'S NOT YOUR FAULT. IT WOULD HAVE HAPPENED SOONER OR LATER.

I HAVE TO ADMIT, THOUGH, I'M PRETTY SHOCKED..

WHY? DON'T YOU THINK IT WAS FAIR?

YEAH, BUT I CAN'T GET OVER HOW QUICKLY JUSTICE WAS SERVED!

WELL, THOSE COMPUTERS TODAY ARE PRETTY AMAZING..

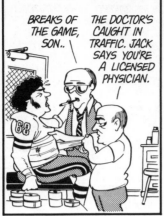

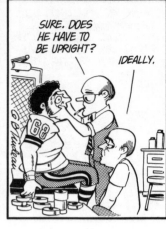

SO HOW'S EDDIE DOING, KID?

HE'S OUT FOR THE SEASON. AS ARE BOTH OF THE GUYS HE CLOTHESLINED.

SIR, I MAY BE A LITTLE OLD-FASHIONED, BUT ALL THESE OVER-AMPED PLAYERS BASHING EACH OTHER'S BRAINS OUT.. CAN THAT BE GOOD FOR THE GAME?

IT'S THE OWNERS, SON. THEY'RE BLIND TO THE PROBLEM. WITHOUT URINE TESTS, WHAT CAN I DO?

I DON'T KNOW, SIR, BUT RIGHT NOW YOU'RE PUTTING A LOT OF GUYS IN THE HOSPITAL!

HEY, LOOK, CHOIR BOY..

SIR, I'VE DECIDED TO GO TO THE PAPERS.

GO TO THE PAPERS? ARE YOU MAD, KID? YOU WANT TO GET THE WHOLE FRONT OFFICE BUSTED?

WELL, NO, SIR, BUT I JUST CAN'T SIT BY AND WATCH THE GAME RUINED BY HOMICIDAL SPEED-FREAKS!

LOOK, RILEY! THIS IS FOOTBALL! TO QUOTE HARRY TRUMAN, IF YOU CAN'T TAKE THE HEAT, THEN GET THE HELL OUT OF NAGASAKI!

YOU LETTING ME GO, SIR?

WELL, NOW THAT YOU MENTION IT, THAT'S A DAMN GOOD..

"BOY, 15, AXED BY REDSKINS' DRUG DOC."

SIT DOWN, RILEY..

IT'S TOO LATE FOR THAT, SIR.

HELLO?

HELLO, IS THIS RICK REDFERN, ACE INVESTIGATIVE REPORTER FOR THE "POST"?

NOT ACCORDING TO MY EDITOR.

I HAVE SOMETHING FOR YOU, SIR. LISTEN CAREFULLY..

THE INJURIES IN LAST SUNDAY'S REDSKINS GAME? THEY WEREN'T JUST BAD LUCK. THE PLAYER RESPONSIBLE WAS STONED OUT OF HIS GOURD AT THE TIME! INTERESTED?

NOT REALLY. HOW OLD ARE YOU, SON?

I'LL BE IN TOUCH. >CLICK!<

..AND IF YOU WANT TO HEAR THE WHOLE TAWDRY STORY, MEET ME AT ZEIBERT'S AT 12:30 SHARP!

12:30 AT ZEIBERT'S. GOT IT.

I MUST HAVE YOUR WORD, THOUGH, MR. REDFERN. MY IDENTITY MUST BE PROTECTED. I HAVE TOO MUCH TO LOSE.

WELL, OKAY, FELLAH. BUT I DON'T KNOW HOW MUCH OF A STORY THAT WILL LEAVE ME.

DON'T WORRY, THIS STORY WILL WRITE ITSELF.

IT WILL?

"INFORMED SOURCE, 15, ROCKS NFL."

NOT BAD.. HOW WILL I KNOW YOU?

YOUR FOOTBALL ARTICLE SEEMS TO BE CAUSING QUITE A STIR, RICHARD..

YEAH, THAT GUY DUKE SURE DOESN'T TAKE THINGS LYING DOWN.

HE RELEASED A 2,000 WORD REBUTTAL YESTERDAY, AND TODAY HE'S HOLDING A PRESS CONFERENCE IN HIS OFFICE..

HE CLAIMS HE'S EVEN GOING TO PRODUCE THE INJURED PLAYER TO TESTIFY ON HIS BEHALF!

I DUNNO, SIR, HE DOESN'T LOOK SO GOOD..

NURSE! CUT THIS MAN DOWN!

..AND DESPITE MY HEATED PRO-TESTATIONS, EDDIE HAS CRAWLED FROM HIS HOSPITAL BED TO JOIN ME IN OUTRAGED DENIAL OF THIS ALLEGED PIECE OF REPORTING!

THIS ARTICLE REPRESENTS THE SHODDIEST KIND OF JOURNALISM! NAMES, DATES, PLACES ARE **ALL** INACCURATE! EVEN DOSAGES ARE DISTORTED AND TAKEN TOTALLY OUT OF CONTEXT!

AS EDDIE VIGOROUSLY CONFIRMS, THE "CONTROLLED SUBSTANCES" I GAVE HIM IN LAST SUNDAY'S GAME WERE NOTHING MORE THAN COMMON ASPIRIN TABLETS! RIGHT, EDDIE?

MMPHH.

NOW, I HOPE WE'VE HEARD THE LAST OF THIS SILLY EPISODE!

>WHEEZE!< COUGH! COUGH!

WHILE WE'RE ALL HERE, I'D LIKE TO TAKE THE OPPORTUN-ITY TO COMMENT FURTHER ON RED-FERN'S INFLAMMATORY PROSE..

UNNH..

IT IS A SORRY STATE OF AFFAIRS WHEN A POLITI-CAL REPORTER IS SENT TO COVER FOOTBALL, A SUB-JECT HE IS CLEARLY UN-EQUIPPED TO COMMENT ON!

UNNH.. ARRGH!

OBVIOUSLY, IN FOOTBALL PEOPLE GET HURT! BUT IT IS THE RISK OF INJURY THAT MAKES THE GAME GREAT! IT IS THE COURAGE OF ATH-LETES AS THEY..

BONK!

EDDIE, WILL YOU SETTLE DOWN? THIS IS IMPORTANT.

> CHIRP!< CAW! CAW!

>RIBBIT! RIBBIT!<

GOOD EVENING. I'M ROLAND BUR-TON HEDLEY, JR., AND THAT WAS THE SCENE TODAY AT CAMP DAVID, SITE OF JIMMY CARTER'S DAZ-ZLING MIDEAST SUMMITRY!

WHAT REALLY WENT ON DURING THOSE THIRTEEN DAYS IN SEPTEM-BER? JOIN US AS ABC WIDE WORLD OF NEWS TAKES AN IN-DEPTH LOOK AT ..**CABIN FEVER!**

"CABIN FEVER: FOOTPATHS TO GLORY," BROUGHT TO YOU BY..

>CHIRP!< >TWITTER!<

CABIN FEVER

abc Wide World Special Report

CABIN FEVER. FOR THIRTEEN LONG DAYS, IT HELD THE WORLD IN ITS GRIP.

WHAT WENT ON IN THOSE SMALL BUT ATTRACTIVELY APPOINTED COTTAGES AT CAMP DAVID? ABC WIDE WORLD OF NEWS RE-CREATES THE ACTION!

DAY ONE. IT'S A LAZY, WARM AFTERNOON AS PRESIDENT ANWAR SADAT'S HELICOPTER TOUCHES DOWN AT CAMP DAVID..

ROLLIE?

YES, FRANK REYNOLDS IN WASHINGTON. YOU'D LIKE TO ADD SOMETHING?

AS I RECALL, THE MOOD WAS HOPEFUL. BACK TO YOU.

DAY FIVE. THE ISRAELIS CLIMB TO NEW HEIGHTS OF INFLEXIBILITY. BEGIN'S INTRANSIGENCE HANGS OVER THE CAMP LIKE A WET BLANKET.

STILL, OCCASIONAL LEVITY CUTS THROUGH THE GLOOM. DURING AN EARLY MORNING STROLL, BEGIN REMARKS TO CARTER, "THIS PLACE IS LIKE HEAVEN ON EARTH."

THE PRESIDENT, SENSING AN OPENING, OFFERS HIM CAMP DAVID. BEGIN, SENSING A RETIREMENT HOME, ACCEPTS.

IF ONLY FOR A MOMENT, CAMP DAVID RINGS WITH LAUGHTER.

DAY TEN. THE MARCH TOWARD PEACE FLOUNDERS. AS TEMPERS FLARE AND ANTES ARE UPPED, JIMMY CARTER ACTS. A TOP AMERICAN NEGOTIATOR REMEMBERS.

WELL, HE SCHEDULED A MOVIE, "PATTON." IT WAS A RATHER COURAGEOUS ACT OF PROGRAMING, SINCE THE SAME FILM ONCE INSPIRED NIXON TO INVADE CAMBODIA.

THE EFFECT WAS QUITE DIFFERENT ON THE ISRAELIS, THOUGH. AFTER ONE ESPECIALLY GORY SCENE, DEFENSE MINISTER WEIZMAN ROSE AND CRIED OUT, "NEVER AGAIN!" THE IMPASSE WAS BROKEN.

COMING UP: PEACE ON THE RAMPAGE.

AMERICAN NEGOTIATOR, IN YOUR OWN WORDS, DESCRIBE THE MOOD AS DAY THIRTEEN BROKE AT CAMP DAVID. IT WAS ONE OF UNCERTAINTY, WAS IT NOT?

THAT'S RIGHT, ROLAND. EVEN AFTER THE CLIMACTIC SADAT-CARTER MEETING IN ASPEN LODGE, THE SUCCESS OF THE SUMMIT WAS STILL IN DOUBT..

AS SADAT WAS LEAVING HIS CABIN, HE BUMPED INTO THE ISRAELI PRIME MINISTER. OFFERING HIS HAND, HE SMILED AND SAID, "LET US BEGIN, BEGIN."

AND BEGIN REPLIED?

"WE'RE NOT OUT OF THE WOODS YET."

STILL DOTTING THE "i"s, EH?

..AND WITH THE RESTOR-ATION OF THE SINAI CAME THE RETURN OF VITAL OIL FIELDS. IN ECO-NOMIC TERMS, IT WAS A SIGNIFICANT CONCESSION!

REMEMBER, LANGUAGE WAS REALLY THE KEY TO THE NEGOTIATIONS. EACH SIDE HAD ITS OWN TERMINOLOGY FOR DESCRIBING A GIVEN GEO-POLITICAL SITUATION.

FOR INSTANCE, MR. SADAT KEPT REFER-RING TO THE WEST BANK AS AN "IN-ADMISSIBLY OCCU-PIED TERRITORY."

AND MR. BEGIN?

BEGIN CALLED IT "THE LAND OF MILK AND HONEY."

DAIRY PRO-DUCTS? THAT'S A NEW TWIST, ISN'T IT?

TOP AMERICAN NEGOTIATOR, IT WASN'T ALL PEACHES AND CREAM AT CAMP DAVID, WAS IT? IN FACT, YOU HAD YOUR SHARE OF LOW WATER MARKS, RIGHT?

THAT'S RIGHT, ROLAND, I'D SAY THE WORST MOMENT CAME WHEN BEGIN ACCUSED SADAT OF DELIBERATELY ATTACKING WHILE ISRAELIS WORSHIPED FOR YOM KIPPUR IN 1973.

HOW DID SADAT RESPOND?

AT FIRST, WITH SOME DIFFICULTY.

AND THEN?

THEN HE ACCUSED BEGIN OF TRYING TO LAY A GUILT TRIP ON HIM.

DOES SEEM LIKE A BIT OF A CHEAP SHOT..

DAY 15: CAMP DAVID PLUS TWO. THE HIS-TORIC PEACE ACCORDS KINDLE AN OUTPOUR-ING OF PUBLIC ACCLAIM!

FOR CARTER, SUCCESS IS SWEET. HIS STANDING WITH CONGRESS AND WITH THE AMERICAN PEOPLE HAS NEVER BEEN ON FIRMER GROUND.

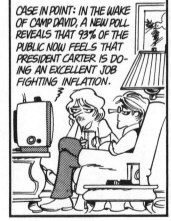

CASE IN POINT: IN THE WAKE OF CAMP DAVID, A NEW POLL REVEALS THAT 93% OF THE PUBLIC NOW FEELS THAT PRESIDENT CARTER IS DO-ING AN EXCELLENT JOB FIGHTING INFLATION.

MOREOVER, 86% NOW AP-PROVE OF HIS HANDLING OF THE LANCE AFFAIR..

WELL, I ALWAYS HAVE.

ME, TOO. HE'S BEEN JUST GREAT!

DAY 16. BEFORE MR. BEGIN DEPARTS FOR HOME, HE GRANTS AN EXCLUSIVE INTERVIEW TO ABC NEWS. HE IS ASKED IF HE HAS ANY PLANS FOR TAKING A VACATION..

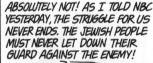

ABSOLUTELY NOT! AS I TOLD NBC YESTERDAY, THE STRUGGLE FOR US NEVER ENDS. THE JEWISH PEOPLE MUST NEVER LET DOWN THEIR GUARD AGAINST THE ENEMY!

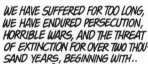

WE HAVE SUFFERED FOR TOO LONG, WE HAVE ENDURED PERSECUTION, HORRIBLE WARS, AND THE THREAT OF EXTINCTION FOR OVER TWO THOU-SAND YEARS, BEGINNING WITH..

ABC NEWS WITHDREW THE QUESTION. BACK AFTER THIS..

WHAT DO THE NEW ACCORDS SPELL FOR MR. BEGIN'S CAREER? IN A FAR-RANGING INTERVIEW, I ASKED THE DOUR LITTLE EX-TERRORIST ABOUT HIS POLITICAL FUTURE..

WELL, AS I TOLD CBS EARLIER, MR. HEDLEY, SOME FRIENDS WILL CRITICIZE ME. BUT THAT IS THEIR RIGHT. IT IS TO BE EXPECTED. THERE IS A PHILOSOPHICAL EXPRESSION FOR THIS..

SWITCHING FROM ENGLISH, MR. BEGIN THEN SPOKE DIRECTLY TO HIS OWN PEOPLE..

.."C'EST LA VIE."

CABIN FEVER PLUS TWO WEEKS. THE DRAMA COMES TO A CLOSE..

THE TWO WEEKS OF DAY-AND-NIGHT SUMMITRY FINALLY CATCH UP WITH AN EXHAUSTED PRESIDENT..

TAKING THE EVENING OFF, MR. CARTER HEADS OUT TO RFK STADIUM, WHERE HE IS THE HONORED GUEST OF THE MANAGEMENT OF THE WASHINGTON REDSKINS FOOTBALL CLUB..

JUST COFFEE. WHY?

FOR THIRTEEN STRAIGHT **DAYS**? C'MON, SIR, YOU CAN TELL ME!

HEY, KIRBY! WHY THE LONG FACE?

I'M AT ODDS WITH MY ERA, ZONKER.

OF COURSE, YOU ARE, KIRBY. WHAT ARE YOU TALKING ABOUT?

GROWING UP IN THE SEVENTIES. I CAN'T SEEM TO ATTACH ANY MEANING TO IT..

HERE WE ARE, ALMOST NINE YEARS INTO THE DECADE, AND THE MAJOR CULTURAL CONTRIBUTION OF THE SEVENTIES IS A FIFTIES REVIVAL CRAZE!

OH, C'MON, KIRBY! WHAT ABOUT DISCO? AND WATERGATE BOOKS?

WELL, OKAY, BUT HOW MANY OTHER BRIGHT SPOTS WERE THERE?

I DON'T QUITE UNDERSTAND, KIRBY. WHAT EXACTLY IS WRONG WITH THE SEVENTIES?

THEY LACK DEFINITION, Z. I DON'T FEEL LIKE I LIVE IN AN ERA I CAN REALLY CALL MY OWN!

OH, I'VE SHOPPED AROUND, OF COURSE. I'VE CHECKED OUT ALL THE TOP-GROSSING PERIOD FILMS, "GREASE," "ANIMAL HOUSE," "COMING HOME," ETC., BUT NONE OF THEM IS REALLY ME. I GUESS YOU COULD SAY I'M A PEG IN SEARCH OF A HOLE!

ROUND OR SQUARE?

DOESN'T MATTER. AS LONG AS IT CAN SUPPORT THE WEIGHT OF MY CONVICTIONS.

BOY, YOU REALLY **ARE** DEPRESSED..

DO YOU REALIZE I HAVE ABSOLUTELY NO MEMORY OF THE FORD YEARS?

HI, KIRBY! WHAT'S UP?

I'M HERE FOR MY FIRST SESSION, ZONK!

SESSION? WHAT SESSION?

ON UNDERSTANDING THE SEVENTIES! DON'T YOU REMEMBER? YOU PROMISED YOU'D HELP ME SELECT AN APPRO-PRIATE NEW LIFESTYLE!

OH, SURE.. RIGHT..

YOU UNDER THE GUN ON THIS?

A LITTLE, YES. I HAVE A BIG DATE ON FRIDAY.

KIRBY, I THINK THE BEST PLACE TO START LOOKING FOR THE SEVENTIES IS RIGHT HERE IN OUR OWN WALDEN LIBRARY!

THEY SAY YOU CAN ALWAYS TELL A CULTURE BY ITS LIT-ERATURE! WELL, WE'VE GOT JUST ABOUT EVERY MOVIE NOVELIZATION AND SELF-HELP MANUAL PUBLISHED IN THE LAST TEN YEARS!

PERSONALLY, I FAVOR THE OUTPUT OF THE NEW SCHOOL OF AMORALITY. LOOKING OUT FOR YOU-KNOW-WHO JUST SEEMS SO SENSIBLE THESE DAYS!

GEE, I DUNNO, ZONK. I'M NOT SURE THAT'S ME..

YOU? WHO CARES ABOUT YOU?

OH, WOW.. YOU REALLY SOUND IN CONTROL OF YOUR LIFE!

OKAY, KIRBY, WHAT ARE WE REALLY AFTER HERE? DO WE KNOW WHAT OUR GOAL IS?

TO LEARN OF OUR ERA'S MOST ENDURING CONCERNS! AS ANDRÉ MAUROIS PUT IT, "IN LITERATURE AS IN LOVE, WE ARE ASTONISHED BY WHAT IS CHOSEN BY OTHERS."

WELL QUOTH! LET'S GET CRACKING!

ZONKER, THAT'S A ZIP CODE DIRECTORY.

HMM.. I THOUGHT THE STYLE SEEMED A LITTLE WOODEN.

THIS IS PRETTY SLOW GOING, Z. I'M NOT SURE I'M MAKING ANY REAL HEADWAY..

WELL, THESE THINGS TAKE TIME, KIRBY.

I KNOW, BUT I WAS HOPING TO WRAP UP MY NEW LIFESTYLE IN TIME FOR MY BIG DATE ON FRIDAY!

HMM..WELL, I SUPPOSE WE COULD OUTFIT YOU WITH SOME SORT OF SHORT TERM POSE..

IT WON'T BE A WHOLLY REALIZED LIFE-STYLE, YOU UNDERSTAND — NOT MUCH MORE THAN A NEW SET OF MANNERISMS — BUT IT SHOULD TIDE YOU OVER.

AND IT'D BE FULLY OPERA-TIONAL?

FOR SURE. ALTHOUGH I'D GO EASY WITH THE DIRECT EYE CONTACT.

VIRGINIA REEL

Q: One of the things that greeted Senator-elect John Warner and his wife, Elizabeth, upon their arrival in the Capital was a series on them in *Doonesbury,* an event which earned its author the censure of the G.O.P. Caucus of the Virginia General Assembly.[1] Any comment?

A: Sure. Better late than never. I had always assumed that the State of Virginia would spare itself the embarrassment of sending the Warners to Washington, but I'm as hopeless a handicapper as I am an optimist. Having missed the boat, I settled for a recap of some of the highlights of the campaign.[2] From the beginning, Warner's deployment of his assets, which is to say his wife and his money, was an absolute marvel, although losing the primary, as he somehow managed to do, was one of those things which gives opportunism a bad name. Fortunately, Providence interceded. His opponent was killed in an airplane crash, and John redeemed himself by immediately volunteering to replace him. Talk about your early bird...

[1]According to the AP, the motion's sponsor, State Senator Wiley Mitchell, announced, "I don't think we should sit placidly by and let the gnomes of the world run over us without expressing indignation."

[2]Warner later told the *Washington Post,* "The facts in the strip are totally false and inaccurate. Oh, I'm not going to pick them out. The people of Virginia know the facts."

You are cordially invited to a Media Event in honor of Senator and Mrs. Elizabeth Taylor

GOOD GOD, HONEY! DO YOU HAVE ANY IDEA HOW **EARLY** IT IS?

YES, SIR, BUT IT COULDN'T WAIT..

I'M JUST ABOUT TO GO INTO MY FOREIGN POLICY SEMINAR WITH PROFESSOR KISSINGER! I NEED YOUR ADVICE..

MY ADVICE? ON WHAT?

WELL, ON WHAT SORTS OF THINGS I SHOULD OR SHOULDN'T BRING UP IN CLASS.

WHAT'D YOU HAVE IN MIND?

WELL, LIKE, IS HE STILL SENSITIVE ABOUT BEING A WAR CRIMINAL?

HELL, NO! HE'S **USED** TO BEING KIDDED ABOUT IT!

TELL ME, FELLOW STUDENTS, IS THERE ANYTHING SPECIAL I SHOULD KNOW ABOUT PROFESSOR KISSINGER?

NOT REALLY. JUST TRY NOT TO TAKE HIM TOO SERIOUSLY. GOD KNOWS **WE** DON'T.

I'M TOLD HE HAS A WONDERFUL SENSE OF HUMOR, THAT HE'S ALWAYS QUIPPING AND TELLING JOKES.

HENRY? JOKES AND QUIPS?

YEAH, LIKE THE ONE HE TELLS ABOUT WANTING TO BE "BORN AGAIN," ONLY THIS TIME IN THE U.S. SO HE'D QUALIFY FOR THE PRESIDENCY!

I'M AFRAID THAT'S NO JOKE, MISS.

IT'S NOT? BUT I WAS TOLD IT WAS HYSTERICAL.

GOOD MORNING. IN TODAY'S READING..

DOC! WHERE ARE YOUR MANNERS? WE HAVE A NEW CLASSMATE!

WHAT'S THAT, MR. WEINBURGER?

SAY HELLO TO MS. HUAN, DOC! FRESH OFF THE BOAT FROM THE PEOPLE'S REPUBLIC!

WELCOME TO OUR CLASS, MS. HUAN. IN LIGHT OF THE RECENT INITIATIVES BETWEEN OUR TWO NATIONS, IT IS A SPECIAL HONOR.

FOR ME AS WELL, SIR! IT IS A FELICITOUS AND HISTORIC TURN WHICH OUR MINGLED DESTINIES HAVE TAKEN!

IT IS INDEED. NOW, IN TODAY'S READING..

I HOPE YOU'LL LET ME BUY YOU A DRINK AFTER CLASS, SIR.

ALTHOUGH THE RECOGNITION OF CHINA IS A GREAT STEP FORWARD, IT SHOULD BE NOTED THAT THE TERMS TO WHICH CARTER AGREED ARE **IDENTICAL** TO THOSE OFFERED FOUR YEARS EARLIER!

BUT, DR. KISSINGER, COULDN'T THE SAME THING BE SAID ABOUT YOUR 1973 VIETNAM CEASE-FIRE ACCORDS?

NO, MISS HUAN, THE TWO ARE **NOT**..

NOT COMPARABLE. YOU'RE RIGHT, SIR. FORGIVE ME, I'D LIKE TO BACK OFF THAT ANALOGY.

YOU WOULD?

YES, SIR. I WAS JUST TESTING THE LIMITS OF YOUR AUTHORITY. CARRY ON.

MAY I JUST SAY HOW DEEPLY HONORED BOTH OF US ARE TO BE HERE TONIGHT. IT'S THE CULMINATION OF A DREAM!

WE HAD A TOUGH RACE. BUT HAPPILY THE VOTERS OF THE STATE OF VIRGINIA KNEW ME AND THEY KNEW WHAT I STOOD FOR, EVEN WHEN I MYSELF WASN'T SURE.

AS THOSE OF YOU WHO ARE IN POLITICS KNOW, YOU CAN'T **BUY** THAT KIND OF SUPPORT, ALTHOUGH WE CERTAINLY DID OUR LEVEL BEST!

IT IS THUS WITH GREAT PRIDE THAT I INTRODUCE MY HUSBAND, JOHN WARNER!

WELL DONE! ADMIT IT, DICK, SHE HANDLES HERSELF SUPERBLY!

THANK YOU, ELIZABETH! IF I MAY, I'D LIKE TO MAKE A TOAST TO OUR NEW FRIENDS!

AS YOU KNOW, WE HAD ORIGINALLY INTENDED TO SPEND THE FALL "EATING OUR WAY ACROSS FRANCE," AS ELIZABETH LIKES TO PUT IT..

BUT FATE INTERVENED, DUTY CALLED, AND NOW HERE WE ARE IN WASHINGTON, ATTENDING WONDERFUL PARTIES!

SO LET'S DRINK TO **FUTURE** PARTIES! AND TO THE SENATE, TOO!

"THE SENATE, TOO?"

YOU WERE RIGHT. HE DOES HAVE A SERIOUS SIDE.

GOOD MORNING, FRONT DESK.

YEAH, THIS IS MR. DUKE. WHERE AM I?

UH..YOU'RE AT THE RAMADA INN IN MIAMI, SIR.

MIAMI? OH, C'MON, WHAT THE HELL WOULD I BE DOING IN MIAMI?

I WOULDN'T KNOW, SIR. MAYBE THE SUPER BOWL. IS EVERYTHING OKAY?

OKAY? ARE YOU GOING TO PRETEND YOU DON'T KNOW THERE'S AN OVERTURNED GOLF CART IN MY BATHROOM?

THIS MUST BE ROOM 402.

LISTEN, THIS PLACE IS FILTHY! I WANT TO CHECK OUT!

IT'S THE BELLBOY, SIR. I'VE GOT THE REST OF YOUR ORDER, SIR..

ORDER? WHAT ORDER?

THE CASE OF GIN, SIR. AND THE GRAPEFRUIT AND THE BADMINTON NETS YOU WANTED!

BADMINTON NETS? I ORDERED BADMINTON NETS?

UH..YES, SIR. YOU SAID YOU WERE CONDUCTING SOME SORT OF EXPERIMENT!

EXPERIMENT? LOOK, I DON'T KNOW WHAT'S GOING ON HERE. JUST SET EVERYTHING BY THE DOOR, OKAY?

OKAY. YOU THROUGH WITH THE GOLF CART YET?

UH..I'M NOT SURE. I NEED TIME TO PIECE THIS THING TOGETHER..

MR. DUKE? IT'S RILEY HERE..

RILEY! WHERE ARE YOU, BOY?

DOWNSTAIRS. THE BELLBOY SAID YOU WERE FINALLY UP, SO I..

RILEY, WHAT THE HELL AM I DOING IN MIAMI? WHAT'S GOING ON? I CAN'T REMEMBER A DAMN THING!

WELL, SIR, THERE WAS AN INCIDENT IN YOUR OFFICE AT REDSKIN PARK. A U.S. MARSHAL WAS INVOLVED..

YOU MEAN, I'M.. I'M..

YES, SIR. YOU'RE ON THE LAM.

DAMN! I KNEW IT! GET UP HERE AND GIVE ME A HAND WITH THESE MATTRESSES!

FOR GOD'S SAKE, SIT DOWN, BOY! BEFORE SOMEONE RECOGNIZES US!

OH, DON'T WORRY, SIR. NO ONE COULD POSSIBLY KNOW YOU'RE IN TOWN..

DON'T BE SO SURE. WHAT DID I DO, ANYWAY?

WELL, SIR, IT ALL STARTED WHEN MR. WILLIAMS FIRED YOU LAST FRIDAY. YOU WOULDN'T LEAVE, SO HE GOT A COURT ORDER TO HAVE YOU REMOVED..

YOUR UNCLE SENT THE DAMN FEDS AFTER ME?

YES, SIR. BUT AS USUAL, WHEN THE MARSHALS TURNED UP, YOU ACTED LIKE YOU'D NEVER EVEN HEARD OF THE U.S. CRIMINAL CODE!

GOOD FOR ME! DAMN THING SHOULDA BEEN SCRAPPED YEARS AGO WHEN...

FORTUNATELY, YOU'RE NOT MUCH OF A SHOT.

MY GOD! YOU MEAN, I GOT INTO A FIRE-FIGHT WITH THE HEAT?

WELL, NOT A FIREFIGHT EXACTLY. YOU JUST SHOT OUT ALL THE FRONT WINDOWS AND TOOK OFF..

THAT NIGHT YOU CALLED ME FROM THE AIRPORT IN A RAGE. YOU SAID YOU KNEW THAT WILLIAMS WAS GOING TO BE AT THE SUPER BOWL, AND THAT YOU WERE GO-ING TO "TRACK HIM DOWN AND GREASE HIM" FOR FIRING YOU.

BEING HIS NEPHEW, I FELT I HAD AN OBLIGATION TO FIND YOU AND NIP THIS SICK, VIOLENT NOTION IN THE BUD! DON'T YOU RE-CALL ANY OF THIS, SIR?

A PLAN.. I MUST HAVE HAD A PLAN.

THINK, SIR! WAS THERE A GUN? I'VE GOT TO TRY TO STOP YOU!

I REALLY CAME ALL THE WAY DOWN HERE JUST TO WASTE WILLIAMS?

SIR, GIVE IT UP! IT CAN ONLY COME TO MORE GRIEF!

GIVE IT UP? KID, IN MY WHOLE LIFE, I..

SIR, IF YOU JUST FORGET THIS STUPID VENDETTA AND GO BACK TO COLORADO, I THINK I CAN PER-SUADE MY UNCLE TO DROP THE CHARGES..

I CAN'T DO THAT, SON, THE REDSKINS NEED..

THE REDSKINS NEED COMPETENT MANAGEMENT, NOT ANOTHER YEAR OF FIXING AND PILLS!

YOU UNGRATE-FUL PUP! DO YOU HAVE ANY IDEA WHAT THE SPREAD WAS BEFORE I AR-RIVED?

I'LL GIVE YOU THREE HOURS. THEN I'M CALLING IN S.W.A.T.!

MR. SECRETARY, THE PEOPLE'S REPUBLIC OF CHINA VEHEMENTLY PROTESTS VIETNAM'S BRUTAL ARMORED ASSAULT INTO THE SOVEREIGN STATE OF KAMPUCHEA!

HANOI'S VILE AND SAVAGE BLITZKRIEG IS AN AFFRONT TO ALL PEACE-LOVING PEOPLES OF THE WORLD, AND SHOULD BE CONDEMNED BY THIS COUNCIL AS THE DESPICABLE, CRIMINAL ACT THAT IT IS!

AMBASSADOR PHRED, HOW DOES VIETNAM RESPOND?

AMBASSADOR PHRED?

SORRY, MR. SECRETARY, I WASN'T PLUGGED IN. WHAT ARE THE CHARGES AGAIN?

MR. SECRETARY, THIS IS AN OUTRAGE! THE AMBASSADOR FROM CHINA HAS NO GROUNDS WHATSOEVER FOR HIS CHARGE OF VIETNAMESE IMPERIALISM!

THE HOSTILITIES IN CAMBODIA WERE THE RESULT OF A POPULAR UPRISING AGAINST A BRUTAL REGIME! VIETNAM PLAYED ONLY A MINOR ADVISORY ROLE!

ADVISORY, MR. AMBASSADOR? THEN PERHAPS YOU COULD EXPLAIN TO THIS COUNCIL THE 100,000 SOLDIERS THAT POURED ACROSS THE BORDER ON DECEMBER 24!

WELL?

LOOK, THEY HEARD SHOTS. THEY WERE CURIOUS.

PHRED, YOUR DEFENSE TODAY OF VIETNAM'S ACTIONS WAS BRILLIANT, JUST BRILLIANT! I KNEW WHEN WE SIGNED THAT FRIENDSHIP ACCORD LAST YEAR YOU'D MAKE US PROUD!

WHY, THANK YOU, MR. AMBASSADOR.

YOU PEOPLE ARE DOING A GREAT JOB FOR US, JUST GREAT! KEEP IT UP!

WHO'S THAT, PHRED?

VIKTOR LOZINSKY, ONE OF OUR SOVIET FRIENDS.

SEEMS NICE.

ACTUALLY, HE'S A PIG, BUT THEY MAKE GREAT TANKS.

MIGUEL! WELCOME BACK! HOW'S EVERYTHING IN MANILA?

PHRED?

TO BE HONEST, PHRED, A BIT TENSE. SPEAKING FOR MY FELLOW DOMINOES, I SHOULD TELL YOU THAT YOUR COUNTRY'S LATEST REAL ESTATE GRAB HAS LEFT ALL OF US A LITTLE JUMPY.

OH, NOW, C'MON, MIGUEL—WITH CHINA CHAFING AT OUR BORDERS, YOU THINK WE NEED THE AGGRAVATION? BESIDES, OUR ASIAN NEIGHBORS ARE VALUED TRADING PARTNERS!

THEN I HAVE YOUR WORD?

WELL, NO, BUT I REALLY THINK YOU'RE BEING PARANOID.

GOOD EVENING. I'M ROLAND HEDLEY BURTON, JR. TONIGHT, ".30/.30" EXAMINES ONE OF THE STRANGEST PHENOMENA IN RECENT POLITICAL HISTORY..

HIS NAME IS EDWARD MOORE KENNEDY. HE IS THE SENIOR SENATOR FROM MASSACHUSETTS. BUT TO HIS THOUSANDS OF DEVOTED FOLLOWERS, HE IS KNOWN SIMPLY AS "TED."

WHO ARE THESE FOLLOWERS? WHERE DO THEY COME FROM? WHAT FORCE DRIVES THEM TO THROW GOOD MONEY AFTER BAD? TONIGHT, ABC WIDE WORLD OF NEWS LOOKS AT..

"THE LIBERAL CULT: THREAT FROM THE LEFT!"

The Liberal Cult
news abc close-up

THE LIBERAL CULT. HUMANE. JUST. FREE-SPENDING. AND UNDER THE GUIDANCE OF ITS CHARISMATIC LEADER, "TED", A MYSTERIOUS NEW FORCE ON THE POLITICAL SCENE!

WHO ARE THESE "LIBERALS"? HOW CAN WE ACCOUNT FOR THEIR CURIOUS APPEARANCE IN AN ERA OF FISCAL RESPONSIBILITY? WE ASKED CONSERVATIVE COLUMNIST DIRK DUPONT.

BEATS ME. I THOUGHT WE HAD THE SUCKERS UNDER CONTROL.

COMING UP: A LIBERAL'S MOTHER RECALLS HER SHAME.

WHAT SORT OF PERSON JOINS KENNEDY'S SO-CALLED "CULT OF CONSCIENCE"? WHAT EXACTLY IS A LIBERAL? ANTIOCH SOCIOLOGIST ALVIN RASHBAUM COMMENTS.

WELL, AS FAR AS WE CAN TELL, "TED" DRAWS HIS SUPPORTERS FROM THE RANKS OF PEOPLE WHO'VE NEVER HAD IT SO GOOD—BLACKS, WORKERS, THE ELDERLY, AND, OF COURSE, NEWLY ARRIVED BOAT PEOPLE.

THE TYPICAL LIBERAL FANTASIZES ABOUT BUILDING A JUST AND EGALITARIAN SOCIETY. WHAT HE DOESN'T UNDERSTAND, OF COURSE, IS THAT THESE THINGS COST MONEY.

IS HE DANGEROUS?

ONLY WHEN HE VOTES. HAPPILY, HE'S DISAFFECTED RIGHT NOW.

WHAT SORT OF SWAY DOES "TED" HAVE OVER HIS FOLLOWERS? I ASKED LIBERAL CONGRESSMAN BART SVIGALS, WHO FLED WASHINGTON DURING LAST YEAR'S OUTBREAK OF TAX-CUT FEVER..

CONGRESSMAN, YOU'VE BEEN IN SELF-IMPOSED EXILE NOW FOR OVER A YEAR, RIGHT?

THAT'S CORRECT, ROLLIE. EVER SINCE THE ROTH-KEMP BILL WAS INTRODUCED.

WOULD YOU RETURN TO CONGRESS IF SENATOR KENNEDY ASKED YOU TO?

YES, I WOULD. I WOULD DO ANYTHING FOR THE MAN.

WOULD YOU.. WOULD YOU OVERSPEND FOR HIM?

LAVISHLY. WITHOUT HESITATION.

COMPASSION. JUSTICE. A FAIR SHAKE. THESE ARE THE PROFESSED GOALS OF THE KENNEDY "CULT OF CONSCIENCE."

AND YET, FOR ALL THE EGALITARIAN POSTURING OF THE LIBERALS, GATHERING SIGNS INDICATE THAT WITHIN THE CULT ITSELF, SOME ARE MORE EQUAL THAN OTHERS!

ABC NEWS HAS JUST LEARNED OF THE EXISTENCE OF AN INNER ELITE, A TIGHTLY KNIT CADRE OF LOYALISTS SO CLOSE TO "TED" THAT THEY'RE ACTUALLY RELATED TO HIM.

REFERRED TO AS THE KENNEDY "CLAN," THEIR EXACT NUMBER IS UNKNOWN..

THE KENNEDY "CLAN". HEIRS TO A POWERFUL LIBERAL LEGACY, THEY ASPIRE FANATICALLY TO A STATE OF TOTAL GRACE.

RESTRICTED DURING THE SUMMER MONTHS TO A FAMILY "COMPOUND," CLAN MEMBERS ARE FORCED TO PRACTICE THEIR BACKHANDS, GROW LONG, UNKEMPT HAIR, AND POSE FOR ENDLESS GROUP PHOTOGRAPHS.

LATER, IN THE FALL, YOUNGER CLAN MEMBERS ARE SENT AWAY TO THE RIGORS OF BOARDING SCHOOL, WHILE OLDER MEMBERS ARE CONFINED TO HARVARD.

DISCIPLINE IS TIGHT. ONLY AFTER THEY HAVE COMPLETED THEIR STUDIES MAY THEY RUN FOR OFFICE.

HAM? THE CONTRACTORS ARE HERE TO START WORK ON THE "NEW FOUNDATION."

GOOD! SEND 'EM IN!

MORNIN', MR. JORDAN.

HI! YOU BOYS FROM THE GSA?

UH.. NO, SIR. WE'RE INDEPENDENTS. BUT WE'RE FULLY BONDED.

THAT'S WHAT THEY ALL SAY. YOU HAD ANY EXPERIENCE IN SHAPING AMERICA'S FUTURE?

WELL, WE ONCE PUT UP A STRUCTURE OF PEACE FOR HENRY KISSINGER.

GREAT.

CAN YOU DO THE JOB, BOYS?

DEPENDS. WHAT KIND OF FOUNDATION ARE YOU FOLKS LOOKING FOR?

SOMETHING SOLID. SOMETHING WE CAN BUILD ON FOR THE FUTURE.

UH-HUH. HOW MUCH YOU GOT TO SPEND?

ABOUT A HALF A TRILLION DOLLARS.

I'LL DO WHAT I CAN. WHAT DO YOU WANT US TO USE FOR A CORNERSTONE?

UM.. I DUNNO. I GUESS OUR STRATEGIC CAPABILITY.

YOU'RE THE BOSS. COURSE, IF THAT GOES, EVERYTHING ELSE WILL, TOO.

I'LL BE PACKED IN A MINUTE, SPRINGFIELD. JUST MAKE YOURSELF COMFORTABLE.

QUITE A PLACE YOU HAVE HERE, MR. DUKE..

THANKS. I BUILT THIS CABIN MYSELF, BACK IN 1963. DID THE DECORATING AND EVERYTHING.

VERY NICE. MAY I ASK WHY YOU KEEP LAND MINES ON ALL THE SOFAS?

YEAH, I WAS TRYING TO TEACH THE DOGS TO STAY OFF THE FURNITURE.

WHAT DOGS?

OKAY, MR. DUKE, YOU'VE BEEN HERE BEFORE, SO I DON'T HAVE TO TELL YOU THAT THIS CONGRESS IS EVERY BIT AS SPINELESS AS ITS PREDECESSORS!

REMEMBER, THE LEGISLATORS WE DON'T OWN OUTRIGHT ARE SCARED TO DEATH OF MAIL! THEY'RE IN YOUR POCKET, MR. DUKE, SO WHEN YOU WALK THROUGH THAT DOOR, WALK **TALL!**

GOTCHA. I DON'T REALLY HAVE TO READ **ALL** OF THESE CRIME-STOPPER STORIES, DO I?

NO, NO, OF COURSE NOT. YOU JUST BE YOURSELF. YOU'RE OUR ACE IN THE HOLE, MR. DUKE!

I AM? WHAT HAPPENED TO THE WIDOW WHO WASTED NINE MUGGERS?

SHE FOLLOWS YOU. YOU'RE OUR NUMBER-ONE GUN!

"..AND IT IS THE POSITION OF THE NATIONAL RIFLE ASSOCIATION THAT WHEN IT COMES TO ARBITRARY SOCIAL CONTROLS, MORE IS LESS!"

"WHAT IS NEEDED INSTEAD IS A SENSE OF RESTRAINT AND FAIR PLAY. IF OUR ONCE PROUD SCHOOLS WERE TO RESUME THE TEACHING OF.."

EXCUSE ME, MR. DUKE..

I WANT TO GET THIS STRAIGHT. IS IT ACTUALLY YOUR VIEW THAT THE ANSWER TO RISING HAND-GUN VIOLENCE IS A RE-NEWED EMPHASIS ON SPORTSMANSHIP?

YES?

EXACTLY. WE ADVOCATE A RETURN TO RESPONSIBLE GUNPLAY.

IN OUR ONCE PROUD — **SCHOOLS?**

"THE NATIONAL RIFLE ASSOCIATION THEREFORE OPPOSES ANY AND ALL LEGISLATIVE ATTEMPTS TO CONTROL OUR CONSTITUTIONAL RIGHT TO BEAR ARMS!"

THAT'S THE END OF OUR PREPARED STATEMENT, MR. CHAIRMAN. I'D BE HAPPY TO ENTERTAIN ANY QUESTIONS.

MR. DUKE, DOES YOUR GROUP'S OPPOSITION EXTEND TO A SIMPLE REQUIREMENT OF SERIAL NUMBERS TO AID POLICE IN IDENTIFICATION?

WHAT'S WRONG WITH DENTAL RECORDS?

I WAS REFERRING TO THE GUNS.

SENATOR, THE POINT IS THAT ONCE YOU HAVE GUN CONTROL, THE ONLY PEOPLE LEFT WITH GUNS ARE CRIMINALS!

WHICH WOULD PREVENT A **GREAT** MANY MURDERS, MR. DUKE!

AS YOU WELL KNOW, ALMOST 70% OF ALL MURDERS ARE COMMITTED AMONG FAMILY MEMBERS OR FRIENDS, AND OVER HALF OF THEM INVOLVE HANDGUNS!

EXACTLY! SO LOOK AT IT FROM THE POINT OF VIEW OF THE VICTIM! WHAT IF **YOUR** WIFE WERE ATTACKING YOU WITH A HANDGUN?

I DON'T FOLLOW, MR. DUKE.

WELL, WOULDN'T YOU WANT TO BE IN A POSITION TO RETURN THE FIRE?

WELL, I..UH..

YOU DON'T HAVE TO ANSWER THAT, JIM.

THE QUESTION WE ARE FACING, THEN, MR. DUKE, IS WHETHER THE WISHES OF 80% OF THE AMERICAN PEOPLE WILL AGAIN GO UNHEEDED..

I CANNOT SPEAK FOR MY COLLEAGUES, BUT I FOR ONE AM **FED UP** WITH YOUR DEADLY LOBBY AND ITS FANATICAL DEFENSE OF A TRAGIC AND UNCONSCIONABLE PUBLIC POLICY!

I SEE.

SHALL I PUT YOU DOWN FOR A MILLION POST CARDS, THEN, SENATOR?

DON'T TRY TO INTIMIDATE **ME**, MR. DUKE!

WE'RE BACK TALKING WITH DR. ALI MAHDAVI, '74, ON LEAVE FROM THE IRANIAN REVOLUTIONARY TRIBUNAL, AND HERE ON CAMPUS FOR HIS FIFTH REUNION!

DR. MAHDAVI, FOR OVER A YEAR NOW, AMERICANS HAVE BEEN HEARING ABOUT THE DARK, SINISTER SIDE OF IRAN'S BEARDED HOLY MAN.

I WONDER IF YOU COULD TELL US SOMETHING OF THE OTHER SIDE, THE HUMAN SIDE..

SUCH AS?

WELL, LIKE WHAT DO BEARDED HOLY MEN HAVE FOR BREAKFAST?

SHAHS. IS THIS GOING TO TAKE LONG?

DR. MAHDAVI, HOW DO YOU RESPOND TO CRITICISM THAT YOUR NEW REVOLUTIONARY GOVERNMENT IS RAPIDLY BECOMING THE WORSE OF TWO EVILS?

IT HAS BEEN CHARGED, FOR INSTANCE, THAT THE AYATOLLAH'S ISLAMIC REPUBLIC IS, IN EFFECT, RETURNING IRAN TO THE 14TH CENTURY!

WELL, YES, THAT WAS THE ORIGINAL PLAN, BUT IT IS ENTIRELY POSSIBLE THERE WILL BE SOME COMPROMISE ON THE EXACT ERA.

YOU MEAN, THERE'S A NEW TARGET DATE?

YES, SOME OF US ARE TRYING TO GET IT MOVED UP TO THE AGE OF VOLTAIRE.

AS YOU KNOW, DR. MAHDAVI, IN RECENT WEEKS, THERE HAS BEEN AN OUTPOURING OF PROTEST FROM IRANIAN WOMEN OVER THE ALL-COVERING "CHADOR," WHICH THEY SEE AS A SYMBOL OF ISLAMIC SEXISM.

WILL THE AYATOLLAH RESPOND TO THIS NEW..

IT HAS ALREADY BEEN RESOLVED. THE RULE ABOUT THE CHADOR WAS BEING TAKEN TOO LITERALLY.

THE AYATOLLAH DOES NOT DISAPPROVE OF OTHER FORMS OF DRESS, AS LONG AS THEY ARE MODEST. WHAT HE DOES OBJECT TO ARE SKIRTS AND GOWNS, THE GARMENTS OF PROSTITUTES!

I SEE. HOW ABOUT THE ANNIE HALL LOOK?

IF WORN WITH A VEIL, FINE.

DR. MAHDAVI, ABOUT HOW FAR CAN WE EXPECT THE NEW IRAN TO TAKE THE EXPULSION OF THE OLD WESTERN PRESENCE?

IT WILL BE COMPLETE. IT WILL BE TOTAL. THE IMMORALITY OF YOUR CULTURE HAS NO PLACE IN IRANIAN SOCIETY!

IT IS SOMETHING WE **CANNOT** COMPROMISE ON! WESTERN INFLUENCES AND CUSTOMS WILL SIMPLY NOT BE TOLERATED! OFFENDERS HAVE ALREADY BEEN PUT TO DEATH!

WHAT? YOU'VE **SEEN** THIS?

SEEN IT? I PERSONALLY CONDEMNED TWO JOGGERS.

DR. MAHDAVI, YOU AND MANY OTHER AMERICAN-EDUCATED IRANIANS HAVE COME A LONG WAY IN THE LAST YEAR — FROM GRADUATE SEMINAR ROOMS TO THE CORRIDORS OF POWER..

HOW DO YOU FEEL ABOUT YOUR REMARKABLE CHANGE OF FORTUNE?

OUR REVOLUTION HAS A SLOGAN WHICH SPEAKS TO THAT. IT IS THIS: "ALLAHU AKBAR!"

WHICH MEANS?

IT MEANS, "GOD IS GREAT."

HOW TRUE! WE'LL BE BACK AFTER THIS!

OR, MORE LOOSELY, "WE'RE NUMBER ONE."

WELL, THAT'S IT FOR TODAY, BOYS AND GIRLS! WE'VE BEEN CHATTING WITH ALUMNUS DR. ALI MAHDAVI ABOUT HIS WORK ON IRAN'S NEW ISLAMIC COURT!

DR. MAHDAVI WILL BE GOING FROM HERE TO HIS CLASS REUNION, WHERE YOURS TRULY WILL BE ONCE AGAIN TENDING BAR!

THANKS FOR BEING WITH US, DR. MAHDAVI. WE CERTAINLY WANT TO WISH YOU AND YOUR GOVERNMENT THE BEST OF LUCK WITH YOUR NEW EXPERIMENT IN HOLY FASCISM!

THANK YOU.

SO UNTIL TOMORROW, BUCKAROOS, THIS IS..

HOLY WHAT?

HOW DO YOU WANT YOUR COFFEE, MR. HALBERSTAM?

BLACK, JOANIE, VERY BLACK, UTTERLY WITHOUT CREAM AND SUGAR!

AS I TOLD JOANIE ON THE PHONE, I'VE ALWAYS WANTED TO MEET YOU, RICHARD RATHBONE REDFERN. DICK. EVERYONE CALLS YOU DICK, RIGHT?

WHATEVER, YOU'RE AN AWESOME FIGURE ON THE LANDSCAPE, BIG, VERY BIG, ONE OF THE STAGGERING SUCCESS STORIES OF OUR BUSINESS...

NO, RICK.

JOANIE, I THINK YOU SHOULD HEAR THIS.

SHE ALREADY KNOWS. HER INTUITION IS EXTRAORDINARY, ALMOST GOD-LIKE.

YOU KNOW, DICK, WHEN I THINK OF YOUR NEW YORK GLORY DAYS BACK ON THE OLD "TRIBUNE," IT JUST SENDS CHILLS UP MY SPINE.

THOSE WERE THE DAYS, ALL RIGHT.

WERE THEY EVER! I DON'T THINK I'LL EVER FORGET YOUR COLUMNS, HOW YOU USED TO FILL THEM WITH ANECDOTES..

THEY WERE BIG, GLISTENING ANECDOTES, VERY MOVING, VERY BRIGHT, ANECDOTES THAT PILED ONE UPON ANOTHER TO FORM A SPRAWLING MOSAIC OF OUR TIMES, THAT WAS HOW BRILLIANT THEY WERE.

OF COURSE, I WAS ONLY STAMPS EDITOR THEN.

NO MATTER. YOU OWNED THE TOWN.

OKAY, THAT BRINGS US UP TO THE LONG, HOT SUMMER OF '68. THAT'S WHEN YOU WERE SENT TO WASHINGTON TO COVER RESURRECTION CITY, RIGHT?

UM.. YEAH, THAT'S RIGHT..

AND IT WAS THERE THAT YOU BECAME SOMETHING OF A DEITY TO YOUR COLLEAGUES, THEY WERE IN AWE OF YOU, BUT THAT DID NOT LESSEN YOUR DEDICATION, IT INCREASED IT, RIGHT?

I JUST DIDN'T KNOW ANY OTHER WAY, DAVID.

OF COURSE, YOU DIDN'T. GOD, YOU LOVED YOUR WORK!

DAVID, BEFORE WE GO ON, I GOTTA ASK YOU—DO YOU REALLY BELIEVE IN THIS JOURNALIST-AS-STAR NONSENSE?

GOD, NO! IT'S THE WORST THING THAT CAN HAPPEN TO BOTH JOURNALISM AND THE PUBLIC!

BUT YOUR BOOKS ARE A MONUMENT TO JUST THAT ADULATION!

MAYBE. DEBATABLE. SUBJECT TO DEBATE. BUT I THINK I SEE YOUR POINT..

WHAT YOU'RE SAYING IS THAT THE CELEBRATION OF THE JOURNALIST IS CORRUPTING, THAT WHEN HE BECOMES BIGGER, MUCH BIGGER, THAN HIS STORY, IT DOES NOT HEIGHTEN HIS EFFECTIVENESS, IT DIMINISHES IT, RIGHT?

EXACTLY. TAKE WOODWARD AND BERNSTEIN..

GODS. I KISS THEIR GUCCIS.

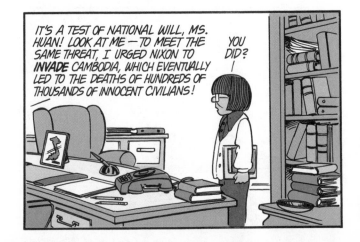

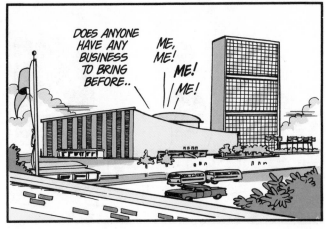

RIINGG!

REACH OUT! REACH OUT! AND *TOUCH* SOMEONE!

HELLO?

LACEY? JOHN WARNER HERE.

WHY, HELLO, DEAR! HOW NICE TO HEAR FROM YOU! ARE YOU AND ELIZABETH HAVING UNE AUTRE SOIREE?

NO, NO, SERIOUS BUSINESS THIS TIME, LACEY..

AS YOU MIGHT HAVE HEARD, I'M HELPING SPEARHEAD THE MOVEMENT TO RESTORE THE FEDERALLY FUNDED GUN CLUB PROGRAM. IT'S MY FIRST BIG INITIA- TIVE AND I NEED YOUR HELP.

BUT, JOHN, DEAREST, YOU HAVE TO BE A MEMBER OF THAT DREARY NRA TO EVEN PARTICIPATE IN THE PROGRAM. IT AMOUNTS TO A DIRECT SUBSIDY!

WELL, NOW, I KNOW IT LOOKS THAT WAY..

..BUT WITHOUT THOSE 300 ROUNDS OF FREE AMMUNITION, THE AVERAGE AMERICAN CAN'T *AFFORD* TO LEARN HOW TO USE AN M-1 TO DEFEND HIS HOME OR CAMPER AGAINST ENEMY FOOT SOLDIERS DURING TIME OF WAR!

YOU CERTAINLY KNOW HOW TO PICK YOUR ISSUES, JOHN.

WELL, I'VE BEEN WORKING ON MY STATURE PROBLEM..

GBTrudeau

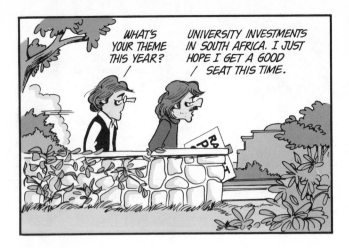

Panel 1: IT'S GOOD TO SEE YOU AGAIN, DUANE. IT'S BEEN TOO LONG. / TELL ME ABOUT IT. WHY IS IT THAT PUBLIC SERVANTS NEVER GET TO SEE THEIR FRIENDS?

Panel 2: I'M AFRAID I WOULDN'T KNOW. HOW'S EVERYTHING OVER AT THE DEPARTMENT OF SYMBOLISM? / WELL, THAT'S WHY I WANTED TO SEE YOU, RICK. I'M ABOUT TO RESIGN AS SECRETARY.

Panel 3: **RESIGN?** THE FAIR-HAIRED BOY OF THE CARTER ADMINISTRATION? WHATEVER **FOR?** / TRY TO STAY CALM, BUDDY. I'VE BEEN OFFERED A JOB AS EXECUTIVE SYMBOLIST TO JERRY BROWN.

Panel 4: OH, DUANE.. / RICK, IT'S A CHANCE TO WORK WITH SOME OF THE MOST IMPORTANT RHETORICAL QUESTIONS OF OUR TIME!

Panel 5: ALL RIGHT, DUANE, WHAT GIVES? / THIS WILL HAVE TO BE OFF THE RECORD, OKAY, RICK? I DON'T WANT TO EMBARRASS JIMMY BEFORE MY FORMAL RESIGNATION..

Panel 6: OKAY, OKAY. NOW, WHAT'S THE DEAL? WHY ARE YOU SKIPPING? / IT'S THE SYMBOLS PROGRAM. IT'S GONE COMPLETELY TO HELL.

Panel 7: I CAN'T FIGURE IT OUT, RICK. WE GOT OFF TO SUCH A MAGNIFICENT START! THE CARDIGAN, THE STROLL, THE TREE HOUSE! BUT LATELY, IT'S ALMOST AS IF JIMMY'S COMMITMENT TO SYMBOLS IS ONLY .. ONLY..

Panel 8: SYMBOLIC? / YOU DON'T KNOW HOW HARD IT IS TO LIVE WITH THAT KIND OF IRONY.

Panel 9: LOOK, DUANE, I CAN UNDERSTAND YOUR DISENCHANTMENT WITH CARTER, BUT WHY JUMP TO JERRY BROWN? / IT'S HIS SYMBOLS, RICK. HIS PACKAGE IS THE BEST!

Panel 10: YOU SEE, RICK, OUR PROBLEMS IN THIS COUNTRY HAVE BECOME SO UNMANAGEABLE THAT THE ONLY PRACTICAL WAY TO RESPOND TO THEM IS ON A SYMBOLIC LEVEL.

Panel 11: BROWN UNDERSTANDS THIS A LOT BETTER THAN JIMMY. I'M PROBABLY BEING UNFAIR, I MEAN, MAYBE IT'S JUST THE OFFICE, BUT DAMMIT, RICK, THE MAN KEEPS TRYING TO ADDRESS THE ISSUES!

Panel 12: YES, WE'VE ALL NOTICED THE CHANGE. / I FEEL LIKE I DON'T EVEN **KNOW** HIM ANYMORE!

Panel 13: RICK, I DON'T SEE WHY YOU'RE SO PUT OUT BY BROWN. THE GUY'S BEEN A **VERY** PROGRESSIVE FORCE IN CALIFORNIA! WHY, LOOK AT THE FARMWORKERS' BILL HE INTRODUCED!

Panel 14: DUANE, I HATE TO BURST YOUR BUBBLE, BUT CHAVEZ HAD THE FARMWORKERS SO WELL ORGANIZED THAT BROWN HAD NO CHOICE.

Panel 15: THE ONLY REASON HE WROTE THE BILL, WHICH WAS NO DIFFERENT FROM CHAVEZ'S, WAS SO THAT **HE** COULD TAKE THE CREDIT FOR IT! / YOU REALLY BELIEVE HE'S THAT CYNICAL?

Panel 16: DUANE, WHO GAVE US, "BLACKS ARE THE WRONG SYMBOL FOR THE 1970's"? / HEY, C'MON, MAN, THEY **HAVE** BEEN QUIET. HE WAS JUST TEASING THEM!

DUANE, ARE YOU SURE YOU'VE THOUGHT THIS THROUGH? I MEAN, WE'RE TALKING ABOUT THE TOP FLAKE IN THE COUNTRY!

WELL, THAT'S JUST ONE VIEW, RICK..

DUANE, LISTEN TO ME..

LOOK, WHY DON'T YOU COME OUT AND SEE FOR YOURSELF? JERRY'S HAVING A PRESS CONFERENCE NEXT WEEK AT THE CALIFORNIA INSTITUTE FOR THE MELLOW.

WHAT FOR?

WELL, I'M NOT REALLY IN A POSITION TO TELL YOU WHAT HE'S ANNOUNCING, BUT I THINK YOU CAN GUESS.

ANOTHER CHANGE OF MIND?

LET'S JUST SAY HE WANTS TO GET SPACESHIP AMERICA MOVING AGAIN.

THIS TRIP IS PROBABLY REAL NECESSARY, HUH, RICK?

WELL, IT IS. I THINK BROWN IS BECOMING AN IMPORTANT STORY..

CAN'T YOU JUST MAKE SOME PHONE CALLS?

PHONE CALLS? JOANIE, I'M A PROFESSIONAL!

BESIDES, HOW CAN I BE SURE THAT JERRY BROWN IS STILL THE MOST CYNICAL MAN IN AMERICA IF I DON'T GO OUT THERE AND SEE FOR MYSELF?

YOU'RE OBSESSED WITH FAIRNESS, AREN'T YOU, RICK?

HAVE TO BE. THERE'S TOO MUCH AT STAKE.

LADIES AND GENTLEMEN, ON BEHALF OF THE CALIFORNIA INSTITUTE FOR THE MELLOW, I'M PROUD TO PRESENT OUR OWN GOVERNOR JERRY BROWN!

THANK YOU VERY MUCH. ARE ALL THE NETWORKS HERE YET?

CHANNEL TWO'S TRUCK BROKE DOWN, GOVERNOR. THEY'LL BE A LITTLE LATE.

OKAY, WE'LL JUST HAVE TO WAIT, THEN.

GOVERNOR, ARE YOU PLANNING ON ANNOUNCING YOUR CANDIDACY FOR THE PRESIDENCY TODAY?

NO. I'M GOING TO BE CREATING A CONTEXT FOR MY CANDIDACY.

I HEAR YOU. COULD WE GET A SHOT OF IT WHEN YOU'RE FINISHED?

GOVERNOR BROWN, WHY WILL YOU ONLY ANNOUNCE A "CONTEXT" FOR YOUR CANDIDACY?

THIS IS AN ERA OF LIMITATIONS. I DON'T THINK PEOPLE WANT FORMAL DECLARATIONS ANYMORE.

WILL THAT APPLY TO YOUR PROGRAM AS WELL?

IN THE ELECTRONIC GLOBAL VILLAGE, PROGRAMS ARE UNIMPORTANT. THEY'RE JUST WORDS. APPEARANCES ARE THE NEW REALITY.

THEN IT'S TRUE THAT YOUR IDEA OF A SOCIAL WORKER IS A T.V. REPAIRMAN?

I DON'T THINK THAT QUESTION RISES TO THE LEVEL OF WHATEVER NETWORK YOU FRONT FOR.

GOVERNOR, IF WE WERE TO TURN OFF THE CAMERAS, WOULD YOU EXIST?

I DON'T WANT TO SPECULATE ON THAT.

GOVERNOR, COULD YOU TELL US A LITTLE A-BOUT WHAT YOU BELIEVE IN?

MY BELIEFS AND CON-VICTIONS ARE WHAT THE PEOPLE CHOOSE TO PROJECT ON ME. I SEE NO NEED FOR ANY OF MY OWN..

BUT WITHOUT CONVICTIONS, HOW CAN YOU ADDRESS SO-CIAL NEEDS?

THERE'S NO SUCH THING AS SOCIAL NEEDS. THERE ARE ONLY POLITICAL PRESSURES. I PRO-MISE TO RESPOND TO ALL OF THEM.

THE PROBLEM IS THIS: WE HAVE A LEADERSHIP CRISIS IN THE CONTROL TOWER OF SPACESHIP AMERICA. THE PEOPLE WANT A LEADER. A LEADER TODAY IS SOMEONE WHO WILL REP-RESENT THEIR EVERY WHIM.

I THOUGHT THAT WAS A FOLLOWER.

THE LAST SHALL BE FIRST. THE FIRST SHALL TAKE NEW HAMPSHIRE.

GOVERNOR, FOR SYMBOLIC PURPOSES, YOU HAVE GONE TO SOME PAINS TO KEEP YOUR PRIVATE LIFE IN THE PUBLIC EYE..

YES, YOU..

VIRTUALLY NOBODY HASN'T HEARD THAT YOU DRIVE AN OLD PLYMOUTH, LIVE IN A SMALL APARTMENT, LIKE MEXICAN FOOD, BUDDHISM, BOB DYLAN, ETC., ETC.

MY QUESTION, GOVERNOR, IS HOW FAR ARE YOU WILLING TO GO IN TRANSFORMING YOUR PRIVATE LIFE INTO NOTHING BUT AN ONGOING PRESS RELEASE?

YOU WANT TO HANDLE THAT ONE, LINDA?

OH, WOW.. NO.

GOVERNOR BROWN, IF I MAY JUST FOLLOW UP ON THAT QUESTION ABOUT YOUR BOX OFFICE PRIORITIES..

WOULD YOU SAY THAT EVEN THE FUTURE OF YOUR RELATIONSHIP WITH MS. RONSTADT IS RESPONSIVE TO PUBLIC MOOD?

YES, OF COURSE. WHY GET MARRIED WHEN A RECENT POLL SHOWS THAT 90% OF CALIFOR-NIAN VOTERS COULD CARE LESS IF LINDA AND I GOT MARRIED OR NOT?

I'VE GOT A NEW ALBUM COMING OUT, THOUGH.

YES, IT ALL COULD CHANGE.

GOVERNOR, ARE YOU COMMITTED TO ANYTHING BEYOND THE PUB-LIC MOOD? FOR INSTANCE, YOU NOW SUPPORT A BALANCED BUD-GET, BUT LESS THAN A YEAR AGO, YOU BITTERLY OP-POSED PROP 13!

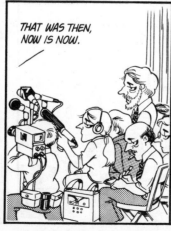

THAT WAS THEN, NOW IS NOW.

UH.. EXCUSE ME, SIR, BUT I'M FROM WASHINGTON. I DON'T KNOW ABOUT CALIFORNIA, BUT BACK EAST THAT WOULD BE A FATUOUS AND CYNICAL ANSWER. I WONDER IF YOU COULD DO BETTER.

EAST IS EAST, WEST IS WEST.

THANK YOU.

SOLDIERS OF MISFORTUNE

Q: Given the uncertainties of the long hostage crisis, wasn't writing about it fairly risky?

A: That's putting it mildly. The day after I finished the series on Reverend Sloan's visit to Teheran, the Desert One debacle broke. I had to kill the whole series, rewrite it, and submit it again after passions over the episode subsided. Strangely enough — considering some of the things I was writing about the students — a number of the strips got through to the hostages.[1] The Iranians had reached a conclusion very familiar to me: that there is no danger of finding anything of substance in the comics.

[1] On January 15, 1980, hostage William F. Keough, Jr., wrote home that "spirits of Americans can be lifted in many ways; thus, to my delight, Trudeau got the message through that the U.S. is very much aware of its citizens, now in their tenth week of imprisonment."

HI, BOSS. WHAT'S UP?

RICK, I WANT YOU TO GET OVER TO THE HILL TODAY AND COVER THE LINKAGE HEARINGS.

WHAT LINKAGE HEARINGS?

YOU KNOW, JACKSON, CHURCH AND COMPANY. THEY'VE JUST FORMED A NEW TASK FORCE TO LINK SALT WITH A SOVIET PRESENCE IN CUBA.

IT'S ALL VERY NOSTALGIC. THEY'VE EVEN NAMED IT AFTER KISSINGER'S OLD CODE NAME FOR THE MAYAGUEZ RESCUE.

GOOD MORNING, OPERATION MANHOOD, MAY I HELP YOU?

GOOD EVENING. TODAY "OPERATION MANHOOD" WENT INTO HIGH GEAR AS SENATORS CHURCH, JACKSON AND BAKER FORMALLY OPENED THEIR SPECIAL LINKAGE HEARINGS.

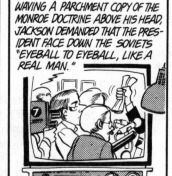

WAVING A PARCHMENT COPY OF THE MONROE DOCTRINE ABOVE HIS HEAD, JACKSON DEMANDED THAT THE PRESIDENT FACE DOWN THE SOVIETS "EYEBALL TO EYEBALL, LIKE A REAL MAN."

IN ANOTHER DEVELOPMENT, THE SENATORS ALSO PLEDGED TO INVESTIGATE NEW EVIDENCE LINKING RUSSIAN SABOTEURS WITH THE SINKING OF THE "MAINE."

FROM THE CHEAP SEATS ON CAPITOL HILL, THIS IS ROLAND HEDLEY, JR.

GENERAL, LET'S GET RIGHT DOWN TO BRASS TACKS! IS THE SOVIET UNION TURNING CUBA INTO A FORTRESS-STATE?

WELL, THE EVIDENCE CERTAINLY SUGGESTS SO, SENATOR JACKSON.

FOR INSTANCE, A RECENT SR-71 FLIGHT BROUGHT BACK SOME AERIAL PHOTOGRAPHS OF A CUBAN MILITARY SUPPLY DEPOT. ONE OF THE PHOTOGRAPHS REVEALED A SOVIET COMMISSARY OFFICER EXAMINING A REQUISITION FORM..

WHEN TRANSLATED FROM THE ORIGINAL SPANISH, THE FORM WAS FOUND TO CONTAIN A REQUEST FOR NEARLY 1,500 CZECH STAPLE GUNS.

STAPLE GUNS? WITH AN OFFENSIVE CAPABILITY?

LET'S JUST SAY THE TECHNOLOGY IS AVAILABLE.

GENERAL, IN YOUR OPINION, DOES THE PRESENCE OF THE SOVIET BRIGADE PRESENT A LEGITIMATE THREAT TO THE SECURITY OF THIS COUNTRY?

SENATOR BAKER, I'D BE LESS THAN CANDID IF I DENIED IT.

MY PERSONAL EVALUATION IS THAT THESE 3,000 RUSSIAN SHOCK TROOPS COULD BE EASILY DEPLOYED TO SPEARHEAD A MASSIVE AMPHIBIOUS ASSAULT AGAINST THE COASTLINES OF FLORIDA, ALABAMA AND SOME PARTS OF MISSISSIPPI.

HAVING ESTABLISHED THESE BEACHHEADS, THE SOVIETS WOULD THEN BE FREE TO FAN OUT ACROSS THE SOUTH, DISRUPTING TRAFFIC, AND EFFECTIVELY CRIPPLING THE TOURIST INDUSTRY SO VITAL TO THE ECONOMY OF THE REGION.

MY GOD! THINK OF THE JOBS!

YES, SIR. AND THAT'S ONLY ONE SCENARIO.

SENATOR CHURCH, IF I MAY JUST MAKE ONE LAST COMMENT..

OF COURSE, GENERAL.

SENATOR, I THINK IT'S FAIR TO SAY THAT IF IT HAD NOT BEEN FOR THE VIGILANCE OF THE U.S. SENATE, THIS MAJOR CRISIS IN CUBA MIGHT HAVE DEGENERATED INTO A MINOR DIPLOMATIC SQUABBLE EASILY HANDLED BY THE STATE DEPARTMENT.

BY REFUSING TO FAN THE FLAMES OF MODERATION, A CALM, NEGOTIATED SOLUTION HAS BEEN NARROWLY AVERTED. THANKS TO YOU AND "OPERATION MANHOOD," THE AMERICAN PEOPLE HAVE BEEN GIVEN ANOTHER CHANCE TO SHOW THAT THEY'RE STILL NUMBER ONE!

THANK YOU, GENERAL, I APPRECIATE THAT.

THANK YOU, SENATOR. AND GOOD LUCK WITH YOUR RE-ELECTION.

GOOD EVENING. TODAY IN WASHINGTON, THE SENATORS BEHIND "OPERATION MANHOOD" WOUND UP THEIR FIRST DAY OF HEARINGS..

AFTER ONLY TWO HOURS OF TESTIMONY, PANEL MEMBERS CAME SURPRISINGLY CLOSE TO AGREEING ON THE HARD-LINE LINKAGE PACKAGE THEY EXPECT TO SEND TO THE WHITE HOUSE.

ONLY LAST-MINUTE PANGS OF CONSCIENCE PREVENTED SENATOR CHURCH FROM ENDORSING SENATOR DOLE'S RESOLUTION CALLING ON THE PRESIDENT TO "LEAD THE COUNTRY TO THE BRINK OF NUCLEAR CONFRONTATION."

THE RESOLUTION WAS SENT BACK TO COMMITTEE FOR REWORDING.

HEY, MIKE! DID YOU KNOW "PLAYBOY" WAS DOING A PICTORIAL ON "THE GIRLS OF THE IVY LEAGUE"?

YEAH, I HEARD. THEIR PHOTOGRAPHER'S ARRIVING ON CAMPUS THIS WEEK.

"$100 FOR FULLY CLOTHED, $200 FOR SEMI-NUDE OR DORSAL, $400 FOR FULL FRONTAL".

THE GUY'S WASTING HIS TIME IF YOU ASK ME.

HEY, C'MON, MIKE, THAT'S A PRETTY GOOD PIECE OF CHANGE!

SURE, BUT SHOW ME A SINGLE WOMAN ON THIS CAMPUS WHO'D TURN SEX OBJECT FOR ANY AMOUNT OF MONEY!

HEY, BOOPSIE!

BUT, OF COURSE. YOUR OWN GIRL FRIEND.

YOU WANT ME TO POSE FOR "PLAYBOY", B.D.?

WHY NOT? YOU'VE GOT THE BOD FOR IT! BESIDES, IT'S AN EASY 400 BUCKS!

GEE, I DUNNO, B.D..

LOOK, I'M TELLING YOU, BOOPSIE, IT'S A HELL OF AN OPPORTUNITY! IF YOUR PICTURE MAKES IT, YOU'LL BE FAMOUS!

ME? FAMOUS?

WELL, SURE! WHY, THAT MAG IS SCOPED EVERY MONTH BY MILLIONS OF GUYS!

GEE.. I WOULD LIKE TO BREAK INTO SHOW BUSINESS..

EXACTLY! AND THIS SURE AS HELL BEATS DRAMA SCHOOL!

B.D., I DON'T LOOK ANYTHING *LIKE* THESE WOMEN! LOOK HOW LONG THIS GIRL'S LEGS ARE!

SHE'S IN HEELS, BOOPSIE. IT'S JUST AN OPTICAL ILLUSION.

I DUNNO, B.D...WHAT IF MY FAMILY FINDS OUT?

NOT A CHANCE! LOOK, BOOPSIE, I KNOW HOW THESE PHOTOGRAPHER GUYS WORK..

AFTER THEY FINISH WITH THE ORANGE LIGHTING AND THE RUBBER BANDS AND THE AIR BRUSHING AND THE ICE CUBES, YOUR OWN *MOTHER* WON'T RECOGNIZE YOU!

"ICE CUBES?" REALLY? ARE YOU SURE?

HELL, YES! THEY EVEN GIVE YOU A NEW NAME IF YOU WANT!

WELL, GOTTA GET GOING. I'M FILLING IN FOR MARK ON HIS SHOW TODAY.

I DON'T SUPPOSE YOU'D BE INTERVIEWING A PHOTOGRAPHER FROM "PLAYBOY"?

HEY.. HOW'D YOU KNOW?

LUCKY GUESS. DID YOU HEAR BOOPSIE'S POSING FOR HIM?

BOOPSIE? POSING FOR "PLAYBOY"? DON'T BE SILLY. I WON'T ALLOW IT.

ZONKER, I DON'T THINK SHE NEEDS YOUR PERMISSION.

SORRY, CASE CLOSED.

ZONKER, SHE'S A BIG GIRL NOW. WE'VE ALL GOT TO LET GO!

WE'RE BACK! I'M ZONKER HARRIS, SUBBING FOR MARK ON "PROFILES ON PARADE," AND I'M TALKING TO "PLAYBOY" PHOTOGRAPHER AND RECRUITER, KURT KLEIG!

MR. KLEIG, I'M SURE A LOT OF OUR LISTENERS ARE WONDERING HOW YOU RECONCILE YOUR LINE OF WORK. FOR INSTANCE, HOW WOULD YOU FEEL IF *YOUR* SISTER OR DAUGHTER TURNED UP IN "PLAYBOY"?

WELL, FIRST OF ALL, MR. HARRIS, YOU SHOULD KNOW THAT WE AT "PLAYBOY" *NEVER* USE DAUGHTERS OR SISTERS IN ANY OF OUR PHOTO SPREADS..!

YOU DON'T? YOU MEAN, THEY'RE ALL MODELS?

ABSOLUTELY, THE LAST THING WE WANT TO DO IS MAKE OUR READERS UNCOMFORTABLE.

OKAY, MR. KLEIG, LET'S START WITH THE HARD QUESTION..

FINE WITH ME. SHOOT!

JUST WHERE THE HECK DO YOU GET OFF TAKING DIRTY PICTURES OF OUR GIRLS?

YOUR GIRLS? NOW, HOLD ON THERE, FELLAH, DON'T YOU THINK YOU'RE BEING A LITTLE PATERNALISTIC?

UH.. NO, I..

DON'T YOU THINK THE WOMEN ON THIS CAMPUS ARE *PERFECTLY* CAPABLE OF MAKING UP THEIR *OWN* MINDS?

BUT YOU DON'T KNOW BOOPSIE!

I DON'T HAVE TO SIT HERE AND LISTEN TO THIS *SEXIST* GARBAGE!

..AND TELL THOSE CLOWNS UP IN SACRAMENTO THAT JERRY'S **SERIOUS** ABOUT HIS PLANETARIUM APPROPRIATIONS BILL!

OKAY, I HEAR YOU.

ALSO, SEE THAT THE DRIVER PICKS UP THE GOVERNOR AT 6:30 TO TAKE HIM TO THE ANTI-NUKE CLAM BAKE.

GOT IT. ANYTHING ELSE?

YES. DO YOU KNOW IF SKYLAB HAS LANDED YET?

NOT SURE. WHY?

JERRY WOULD LIKE TO BE THERE TO MEET IT.

OKAY. I'LL PUT OUT SOME FEELERS.

G B Trudeau

SYMBOLS. DELACOURT HERE.

HI, DUANE, IT'S GRAY. WE'VE GOT A PROBLEM.

NBC HAS BROKEN A STORY THAT'S GIVING US SOME P.R. HEADACHES. THEY'RE CLAIMING THAT JERRY ONCE SOLICITED A $1000 CONTRIBUTION FROM A LOCAL MAFIA BIGGIE.

WELL?

WELL, WHAT?

IS IT TRUE?

THAT'S NOT YOUR DEPARTMENT! I MEAN, OF **COURSE** NOT!

G B Trudeau

LET ME GET THIS STRAIGHT, GRAY— **WHO** EXACTLY DID JERRY SOLICIT THE CONTRIBUTION FROM?

A GUY NAMED SIDNEY KORSHAK. HE'S THE LOCAL LOW-LIFE, AN ALUMNUS FROM THE CAPONE MOB..

UNFORTUNATELY, IT DOESN'T STOP WITH THE CONTRIBUTION. JERRY ALSO TRIED TO CLOSE A RACE TRACK AS A FAVOR TO A STRIKING UNION. GUESS WHO WAS REPRESENTING THE UNION?

COULD BE A COINCIDENCE, RIGHT?

WELL, THAT'S UP TO YOU, DUANE. JERRY WANTS YOU TO WORK UP A P.R. STRATEGY AND MEET HIM AT EL ADOBE FOR DINNER.

GRAY, I DON'T "WORK UP P.R. STRATEGIES." I CREATE SYMBOLS.

SUIT YOURSELF. BUT HE'S GOING TO WANT TO SEE SOME LAYOUTS.

G B Trudeau

GRAY TELLS ME WE'VE GOT A BIT OF A PROBLEM, GOVERNOR.

YEAH, AND IT'S NOT FAIR. I DON'T EVEN **KNOW** THIS CREEP KORSHAK!

YOU DON'T?

OKAY, SO I MAY HAVE RUN INTO HIM A FEW TIMES AT LEW WASSERMAN'S PARTIES.

WHO?

LEW WASSERMAN. HE'S A MOVIE MOGUL. HE HAS TO DEAL WITH KORSHAK TO GET HIS MOVIES MADE.

MOVIES? GOVERNOR, WHAT'S THAT GOT TO DO WITH..

LOOK, THAT'S ALL I KNOW. I WAS IN AFRICA. I'VE GOT WITNESSES.

G B Trudeau

GOVERNOR, IF I'M GOING TO HANDLE THE PRESS ON THIS ONE, I'M GOING TO NEED ALL THE INFORMATION YOU CAN GIVE ME.

NO PROBLEM. I HAVE NOTHING TO HIDE.

GOOD. NOW, WHEN THE NBC REPORTER ASKED YOU WHY YOU SOLICITED $1000 FROM A KNOWN ORGANIZED CRIME FIGURE, HOW EXACTLY DID YOU JUSTIFY IT?

I POINTED OUT THAT EVEN JANE FONDA HAD ONCE BEEN INVESTIGATED BY THE F.B.I.

WHICH IS WHY YOU APPOINTED HER TO YOUR ARTS COMMISSION?

ABSOLUTELY. I BELIEVE THESE PEOPLE CAN BE REHABILITATED.

SO WHAT THEY'RE SAYING IS THAT I TRIED TO CLOSE A HORSE RACING TRACK AT THE BIDDING OF AN UNDISPUTED MOBSTER! ME, A FORMER JESUIT, FOR GOD'S SAKE!

IS IT TRUE, BOSS?

IS WHAT TRUE?

IS IT TRUE THE FIX WAS IN?

THEY MAKE A PRETTY FAIR TACO HERE, DON'T YOU THINK?

BOSS..

WHAT'S "AN UNDISPUTED MOBSTER" REALLY MEAN, ANYWAY? ISN'T THAT JUST A TIRED CLICHÉ?

DUANE, THE BOSS IS REALLY STARTING TO FEEL THE HEAT, BUDDY.

I'M ON IT, GRAY. I CALLED A PRESS CONFERENCE FOR THIS AFTERNOON.

HOW ARE YOU PLANNING TO EXPLAIN JERRY'S ASSOCIATION WITH KORSHAK?

WELL, I THOUGHT I'D SAY THAT BROWN IS INTRIGUED BY THE MAFIA ONLY AS A SOURCE OF IDEAS.

I'LL POINT OUT THAT ORGANIZED CRIME IS ONE OF THE FEW LABOR-INTENSIVE INDUSTRIES TO BE BOTH SELF-REGULATORY AND COST-EFFICIENT.

SO WE ALL HAVE MUCH TO LEARN, ETC.?

EXACTLY. I THOUGHT I'D SHOW SOME FLOW CHARTS.

UH..ROLAND, IF YOU DON'T MIND, I'D LIKE TO GET THIS THING STARTED..

JUST ONE QUICK STAND-UP, BUDDY, AND WE'LL BE OUT OF YOUR WAY!

THIS IS ROLAND HEDLEY, JR., IN LOS ANGELES. TONIGHT, ABC NEWS LOOKS AT A SORDID STORY ABOUT THE TANGLED DESTINIES OF A GOVERNOR, A RACKETEER, AND A MOVIE TYCOON!

IT'S ALSO A STORY OF INFLUENCE AND FIXING, BUT HEY, LET'S LET THE GRAND JURY SORT THAT OUT! FOR NOW, LET'S LISTEN TO BROWN SPOKESMAN DUANE DELACOURT TRY TO DEFEND HIS BOSS!

UH..

THIRTY SECONDS, BUDDY.

ROLLING!

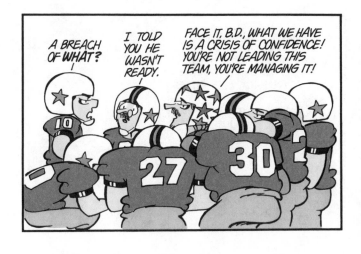

IT'S ABC WIDE WORLD OF NIGHTLY NEWS!

HERE'S FRANK, MAX, PETER AND BARBARA. ENJOY.

GOOD EVENING FOR ABC WIDE WORLD OF NEWS. I'M FRANK REYNOLDS IN WASHINGTON. OUR TOP STORY IS IN DETROIT.

EVEN THOUGH INSTANTANEOUS, NATION-WIDE TRANSMISSION MAKES ANCHOR LOCATION IRRELEVANT, LET'S GO TO MAX ROBINSON IN CHICAGO, ON THE GROUNDS THAT HE'S CLOSER TO THE STORY.

TODAY IN DETROIT, THE BIG THREE AUTOMAKERS ANNOUNCED SHARPLY DECLINING SALES. WHAT EFFECT THAT WILL HAVE ON THE NATIONAL MALAISE REMAINS TO BE SEEN. FRANK?

IN OTHER NEWS, MEXICO HAS ANNOUNCED A TENTATIVE AGREE-MENT WITH THE UNITED STATES ON THE SALE OF NATURAL GAS..

I'D GIVE YOU THE DETAILS MYSELF, BUT PETER JENNINGS IS OUR FOR-EIGN EDITOR, SO TO GET THE STORY IN MEXICO, LET'S GO TO A COM-PLETELY DIFFERENT HEMISPHERE.

GOOD EVENING FROM LONDON..

DUKE? DUKE, ARE YOU OKAY? IT'S ME, BRENNER!

BRENNER? BRENNER, MY MAN-SERVANT?

BRENNER, YOUR CARETAKER. WHAT ARE YOU DOING DOWN THERE, MAN?

CELEBRATING. I'M OFF WELFARE. I CAN AFFORD YOU NOW.

THAT'S GOOD NEWS, MAN. WHAT'S THE JOB?

IT'S CONFIDENTIAL, BRENNER. IN FACT, IT'S SO SENSITIVE, SO CRITICAL, EVEN I DON'T KNOW WHAT IT IS! AS OF TODAY YOU'RE WORKING FOR A MAN ON THE CUTTING EDGE OF HISTORY!

SOUNDS DICEY, MAN. I'LL NEED A DEPOSIT.

BRENNER, YOU JUST WROTE YOURSELF OUT OF MY MEMOIRS.

LOOK, DUKE, BEFORE YOU GO, WE HAVE TO TALK ABOUT FINANCES. I HAVEN'T BEEN PAID IN A YEAR!

NEITHER HAVE I, BRENNER. WE ALL HAVE OUR CROSSES TO BEAR.

DUKE, I'M SERIOUS! IF YOU DON'T PAY ME NOW, I DON'T SEE HOW I'LL BE ABLE TO KEEP..

PAY YOU? PAY YOU FOR WHAT? YOU CALL YOURSELF A CARETAKER? LOOK AT THIS PLACE!

YOU DON'T UNDERSTAND, MAN. SEE, MY OL' LADY IS EXPECTING, AND..

DAMMIT, BRENNER! DON'T DRAG YOUR PERSONAL LIFE INTO THIS! IT'S UNPROFESSIONAL!

OH.. SORRY, MAN, I..

YOU DON'T SEE ME WHINING ABOUT MOTHER'S TUMOR, DO YOU?

YEAH?

DUKE? ANDREWS HERE. LISTEN VERY CAREFULLY. YOU'RE LEAVING TONIGHT FOR THE DENVER AIRPORT..

AT EXACTLY 11:30 P.M., GO TO THE PAY PHONE BEHIND THE AVIS COUNTER. ON THE THIRD RING, PICK UP THE RECEIVER AND ASK FOR "MOTHER"..

NOT SO FAST, BIG FELLAH! I'M NOT GOING ANYWHERE UNTIL I SEE AN ADVANCE! WHERE THE HELL ARE MY KRUGERRANDS?

NICE TRY, DUKE. YOUR GOLD WAS DELIVERED YESTERDAY. WE'VE GOT YOUR CARETAKER'S SIGNATURE.

WHOSE SIGNATURE?

LOOK, DUKE, IF YOU CAN'T KEEP YOUR OWN PEOPLE IN LINE, DON'T BLAME ME!

OKAY, BRENNER, DON'T EVEN BLINK.

DUKE! WHAT ARE YOU DOING, MAN? PUT THAT THING DOWN!

I'M ONLY GOING TO ASK YOU ONCE, BRENNER! WHERE THE HELL ARE MY KRUGERRANDS?

YOUR WHAT? I DON'T KNOW WHAT YOU'RE TALKING ABOUT, MAN!

DON'T GIVE ME THAT, FUZZ-FACE! WHERE'S THE BOX YOU SIGNED FOR YESTERDAY?

THE BOX? I PUT IT IN THE REFRIGERATOR.

THE REFRIGERATOR?

IT SAID "RUSH," MAN. I THOUGHT IT WAS YOUR FRUIT-OF-THE-MONTH CLUB.

LISTEN, ANDREWS, I STILL DON'T SEE WHERE I FIT IN!

THEN LET ME COME TO THE POINT. YOUR MISSION, DUKE, IS TO GET TO "DIPSTICK," OUR OPERATIVE AT THE AHVAZ OILFIELDS!

IT'S A VITAL MISSION, DUKE. WITH THE COOPERATION OF AN INSIDER LIKE HIM, WE'LL BE ABLE TO GET THE OIL MOVING OUT OF IRAN AGAIN!

LET ME GET THIS STRAIGHT. ALL I HAVE TO DO IS FLY TO AHVAZ AND MAKE A PAYOFF? THAT'S THE WHOLE GIG?

AT THE COMPLETION OF WHICH, YOU WILL BE $100,000 THE WEALTHIER, AS PER OUR AGREEMENT.

I LIKE IT. SIMPLE, SAFE..

GOOD. NOW, I HAVE HERE SOME COLOR SWATCHES FOR YOUR PARACHUTE..

PARACHUTE? ME? ARE YOU MAD, ANDREWS?

A SMALL RISK CONSIDERING THE STAKES, DUKE..

MAY I JUST REMIND YOU THAT AT THIS POINT, THE ONLY THING STANDING BETWEEN OUR WHOLE WAY OF LIFE AND ARMAGEDDON IS ONE 42-YEAR-OLD BALDING BAGMAN — YOU!

ANDREWS, HAVE YOU EVER HURLED YOURSELF OUT OF AN AIRPLANE AT 30,000 FEET?

IT'S PERFECTLY SAFE, DUKE. BESIDES, THE IRANIAN AIR FORCE ALMOST NEVER PATROLS AT NIGHT.

NIGHT? HOW AM I SUPPOSED TO FIND THE DAMN TARGET AT NIGHT?

YOU JUST FOLLOW THE TRACERS. LOOK, DUKE, I'D DO IT MYSELF IF IT WEREN'T FOR MY BACK.

I DON'T LIKE THE WAY THIS OPERATION IS SHAPING UP, ANDREWS, I DON'T LIKE IT AT ALL!

IT'S GOING TO BE A PIECE OF CAKE, DUKE. JUST TRUST ME.

TRUST YOU? TRUST JAMES "OBSCENE PROFITS" ANDREWS?

LOOK, YOU'VE HAD A LONG DAY. YOU'LL FEEL BETTER ABOUT IT IN THE MORNING.

NOT BLOODY LIKELY! WHEN ARE WE LEAVING?

NOT FOR A FEW WEEKS. PLENTY OF TIME TO GET YOUR VISA AND PUT YOUR ESTATE IN ORDER.

107

SAY WHAT?

JUST AS A COURTESY TO YOUR FAMILY, DUKE. SO THEY WON'T WORRY.

107

WELL?

THEY LEFT ANKARA ON TIME, "MOTHER." "EAGLE" SHOULD HAVE LANDED IN IRAN NEARLY TWO HOURS AGO.

DAMN HIM! DUKE KNOWS HE'S SUPPOSED TO CONTACT US ON TOUCHDOWN!

MAYBE HIS PARACHUTE DIDN'T OPEN, SIR.

NOT A CHANCE. I PACKED IT MYSELF.

WELL, MAYBE HE DECIDED TO KEEP THE PAYOFF MONEY FOR HIMSELF.

PERHAPS. I WAS HOPING HIS MOTHER WOULD DISCOURAGE THAT.

THAT REMINDS ME. I BETTER CHECK ON HER AIR SUPPLY.

THIS IS ROLAND HEDLEY. IT'S A BLEAK, DARK MORNING HERE IN TEHERAN AS THE ESPIONAGE TRIAL OF FORMER AMBASSADOR DUKE GETS UNDER WAY!

IN THE NEW IRAN, THE ISLAMIC KANGAROO COURTS ARE CUSTOMARILY GAVELED TO ORDER AT AN UNGODLY 4:00 A.M.! TODAY SHOULD BE NO EXCEPTION.

TENSION HAS BEEN MOUNTING HERE ALL WEEK AS..

THE WHOLE WORLD IS *WATCHING!* THE WHOLE WORLD IS *WATCHING!*

AH, HERE COMES THE DEFENDANT NOW!

THE WHOLE.. *THUD!* ‹ ≤ UNH!

THE REVOLUTIONARY TRIBUNAL WILL NOW COME TO ORDER! THE COURT WILL HEAR THE ISLAMIC REPUBLIC OF IRAN VS. AMBASSADOR DUKE!

BAM! BAM!

HAS THE STATE PREPARED ITS CASE?

WE HAVE, EXCELLENCY.

LOOKS IRONCLAD TO ME.

THANKS. SORRY ABOUT THE TYPOS.

NOW, *WAIT* A MINUTE!

"THE PEOPLE FURTHER CHARGE THAT MR. DUKE ENTERED THIS COUNTRY FOR THE EXPRESS PURPOSE OF ESPIONAGE AND BRIBERY."

WHAT IS THE DEFENSE OF THE ACCUSED?

HE MAINTAINS HE'S AN INNOCENT TOURIST.

IS THAT CORRECT, MR. DUKE?

MR. DUKE?

OH, SORRY, YOUR HONOR, I WAS JUST WRITING A FEW POSTCARDS.

THE DEFENDANT, AMBASSADOR DUKE, IS CHARGED HERE WITH HIGH CRIMES AGAINST GOD AND THE ISLAMIC REPUBLIC OF IRAN.

HE IS FURTHER ACCUSED OF ESPIONAGE, BRIBERY, ILLEGAL ENTRY AND POSSESSION OF DRUGS. THE PENALTY IN ALL CASES IS DEATH.

THE EVIDENCE IS OVERWHELMING. I FIND THE DEFENDANT GUILTY AS CHARGED!

WHAT? THE *HELL* I AM!

THE BAILIFF MAY FIRE WHEN READY.

OKAY, *OKAY!* I'M WILLING TO DEAL!

MR. DUKE WAS THEN DRAGGED SCREAMING AND KICKING TO THE GRAVEL ROOFTOP OF THE COURTHOUSE, A POPULAR SPOT IN RECENT MONTHS FOR DISCIPLINING FORMER SAVAK AGENTS.

AS YET, HOWEVER, THERE HAS BEEN NO OFFICIAL INDICATION THAT THE SENTENCE HAS BEEN CARRIED OUT. CERTAINLY THIS REPORTER HAS HEARD NO SHOTS, AND HE HAS KEPT HIS EARS PRICKED.

MOREOVER, THERE ARE NOW REPORTS THAT SENSITIVE NEGOTIATIONS MAY BE UNDER WAY IN A LAST-DITCH ATTEMPT TO SAVE THE FORMER AMBASSADOR'S LIFE.

$500,000! IN GOLD!

$250,000! AND THAT'S MY FINAL OFFER!

YES?

HI! IS MS. CAUCUS HOME?

NO, I'M SORRY, JOANIE'S ALREADY LEFT FOR WORK.

OH. MIND IF I USE YOUR PHONE TO CALL HER?

UH.. MAY I ASK WHO YOU ARE, MISS?

I'M HER DAUGHTER, JOAN, JR.

"JOAN, JR."?

YOU MUST BE MOM'S OLD MAN.

"JOAN, JR.?"

YEAH, CAN I COME IN? I'VE BEEN UP ALL NIGHT ON THE BUS..

UH.. ARE YOU SURE THERE ISN'T SOME MISTAKE HERE, YOUNG LADY?

THIS IS JOANIE CAUCUS'S APARTMENT, RIGHT? WHO ARE YOU?

I'M A FRIEND OF HERS, RICK REDFERN.

GLAD TO MEET YOU, RICK. I TAKE IT MOM HASN'T TOLD YOU SHE HAS A DAUGHTER YET.

LOOK, DO YOU HAVE AN I.D. OR SOMETHING?

SURE. GEE, I HOPE I HAVEN'T SCREWED UP HER STRATEGY.

TELL ME, MISS, HOW LONG HAS IT BEEN SINCE YOU'VE SEEN JOANIE?

ALMOST SEVEN YEARS..

ALL THAT TIME SHE'S BEEN SENDING DADDY CHILD SUPPORT, BUT BASICALLY, SHE'S NEVER BEEN ABLE TO DEAL WITH THE FACT THAT SHE JUST SORT OF SPLIT ON US.

GEE, I.. I DON'T KNOW WHAT TO SAY, MISS. THIS IS SOMETHING OF A SHOCK..

PLEASE, CALL ME JOAN, JR.

RIGHT. I'LL NEED SOME TIME ON THAT ONE.

I UNDERSTAND. CAN I GET YOU A GLASS OF WATER?

POLITICAL MEMOIRS ARE NOTORIOUSLY SELF-SERVING, AND "WHITEWASH YEARS" IS NO EXCEPTION. SO IS THE BOOK OF ANY HISTORICAL VALUE? WE ASKED HISTORIAN LEO PARTCH.

WELL, IT'S HARD TO TELL, REALLY, BECAUSE THERE'S SO LITTLE IN THE LITERATURE TO WEIGH IT AGAINST.

SO FAR THE ONLY BOOKS ON KISSINGER HAVE BEEN WRITTEN BY OBSEQUIOUS T.V. CORRESPONDENTS WHO STILL TREMBLE AT THE HONOR OF ADDRESSING HIM BY HIS FIRST NAME.

FOR THE RECORD, THIS REPORTER HAS NEVER ENJOYED "HENRY" PRIVILEGES. BACK AFTER THIS.

AND SO THE BIG QUESTION AT TIME, INC., IS THIS: WILL SURVIVORS OF THE NIXON-KISSINGER ERA ACTUALLY BE TEMPTED TO PAY MONEY TO RELIVE IT?

700,000 WORDS. 1,521 PAGES. THE 30-MONTH OUTPUT OF KISSINGER'S HANDPICKED MEMOIR STAFF. BY ALMOST ANY STANDARD, "WHITEWASH YEARS" IS A VERY BIG BOOK!

GRANTED, HENRY KISSINGER HAD MUCH TO ANSWER FOR, BUT NEED SO MANY TREES HAVE DIED FOR THE CAUSE? MOST KISSINGER SCHOLARS THINK NOT.

HELL, IT ONLY TOOK ALBERT SPEER 520 PAGES..

THANK YOU, MR. WEINBURGER. ANY OTHER COMMENTS?

JOAN, JR?

HI! YOU MUST BE MY ROOMMATE, CHING!

ALL MY FRIENDS CALL ME HONEY.

PLEASED TO MEET YOU, HONEY. YOU CAN CALL ME J.J.

WELCOME TO COLLEGE, J.J.

THANK YOU.

I SUSPECT YOU WANT TO BE FILLED IN ON THE MEN SITUATION.

WELL, LET ME JUST GET RID OF THE PARENTS FIRST..

ANY WORD FROM YOUR BOYFRIEND YET, HONEY?

NO, AND I FEAR THE WORST.

I KNOW HE WOULDN'T WANT ME TO WORRY, BUT I CAN'T HELP IT. KHOMEINI'S PEOPLE ARE NOTHING BUT A GANG OF COMMON HOODLUMS!

KHOMEINI? WAIT A MINUTE! IS YOUR BOYFRIEND AMBASSADOR *DUKE*?

WE FELL IN LOVE IN THE EMBASSY COMPOUND. ALL OF PEKING WAS ABUZZ OVER IT..

WOW.. HOW ROMANTIC!

WE WERE TO BE MARRIED. I WAS GOING TO OPEN UP A LITTLE RESTAURANT IN DENVER.

WHAT'S IT SAY, ZONK?

"REGRET TO INFORM YOU YOUR UNCLE DUKE HAS BEEN DECLARED LEGALLY DEAD."

"READING OF WILL SCHEDULED FOR MONDAY. PLEASE COME SOONEST TO HELP ORGANIZE PERSONAL EFFECTS. CONDOLENCES. T. BANNON, ATTORNEY-AT-LAW."

GEE.. WHO DO YOU SUPPOSE MOVED TO HAVE HIM DECLARED LEGALLY DEAD?

I'M NOT SURE, BUT I'VE GOT A PRETTY GOOD IDEA!

YOU WANT THE STEREO PACKED TOO, BUDDY?

NO, NO, JUST PUT IT IN THE BACK OF MY VAN.

THIS SIDE UP↑

FRAGILE

© B Trudeau

IS THAT YOU, BRENNER?

HEY, ZONK! GOOD TO SEE YOU AGAIN, MAN!

DUKE

BRENNER, WHAT THE HELL IS GOING ON? WHO HAD DUKE DECLARED DEAD?

IT HAD TO BE DONE SOONER OR LATER, MAN. LIFE GOES ON, YOU KNOW?

DUKE

SO YOU WROTE HIM OFF? JUST LIKE THAT?

WELL, WE WERE THINKING OF A MEMORIAL SERVICE, BUT HIS ATTORNEY AND I FIGURED WE OUGHTA TRY TO KEEP EXPENSES DOWN.

DUKE

AS A COURTESY TO HIS HEIRS, NO DOUBT.

RIGHT. BESIDES, I COULDN'T REMEMBER WHICH CULT HE BELONGED TO.

DUKE

GLAD YOU GOT HERE SO FAST, ZONK. THERE'S A LOT OF STUFF TO SORT THROUGH BEFORE THE WILL READING!

FRAGILE

WHO'S COMING TO THE READING, BRENNER?

A PRETTY HEAVY CROWD, MAN. A GANG OF CREDITORS, A COUPLE IRS GUYS, AND A U.S. MARSHAL.

FRAGILE

A U.S. MARSHAL?

NOT TO WORRY, MAN. I CHECKED IT OUT, AND MOST OF DUKE'S ESTATE IS INADMISSIBLE.

FRAGILE

IMAGINE MY RELIEF.

ALL WE GOTTA DO IS GET THE SERIAL NUMBERS OFF.

FRAGILE

© B Trudeau

FIND ANYTHING INTERESTING YET, MAN?

ARE YOU KIDDING? JUST LOOK AT ALL THIS STUFF!

PARKING TICKETS, EVICTION NOTICES, BETTING STUBS, FOOD STAMPS, BOUNCED CHECKS, REJECTION SLIPS, UNFINISHED MANUSCRIPTS, OVERDUE BILLS..

.. PRESCRIPTION BLANKS, FORGED PASSPORTS.. WHY, BRENNER, THERE'S A RECORD OF FAILURE AND MALFEASANCE HERE THAT SPANS OVER TWENTY YEARS!

YOU THINKING OF EDITING HIS PAPERS, MAN?

I DON'T KNOW IF I COULD DO IT JUSTICE!

© B Trudeau

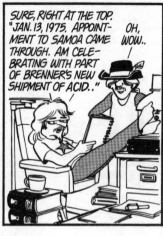

"APRIL 15, 1976. PEKING. INTENSE NEGOTIATIONS ON STATUS OF U.S./CHINA RELATIONS CONTINUE AT GREAT HALL OF THE PEOPLE.."

"TENG IS UNCOMPROMISING ON TAIWAN ISSUE. I MAKE NINE SEPARATE PROPOSALS, INCLUDING GENEROUS CASH SETTLEMENTS, PLUS POINTS. AM REBUKED AT EVERY TURN."

"APRIL 16. TENG REMAINS INTRACTABLE. IN ATTEMPT TO BREAK DEADLOCK, I CALL IN AIR STRIKES ON IMPERIAL PALACE."

"APRIL 17. PENTAGON OVERRULES STRIKES. AM LOSING FACE."

OKAY, IF EVERYONE HAS SOMETHING TO DRINK, I'D LIKE TO GET THIS SHOW ON THE ROAD.

I'M T.F. BANNON, COUNSEL FOR THE FIRM OF TORTS, TARTZ AND TORQUE, AND PERSONAL ATTORNEY FOR AMBASSADOR DUKE.

IT IS MY UNHAPPY TASK TO BE HERE TODAY TO READ THE WILL OF MR. DUKE, WHO IS.. UH.. PRESUMED DEAD AT THIS TIME.

STILL NO WORD FROM THE DECEASED YET, RIGHT?

NOT A PEEP, MAN. LET'S DO IT.

YOU A FRIEND OF THE FAMILY?

YOU MIGHT SAY THAT. I WORK FOR THE INTERNAL REVENUE SERVICE.

REALLY? HAVE YOU KNOWN DUKE LONG?

I WAS FIRST ASSIGNED TO HIS CASE IN 1963.

WOW..

HOW YOU BEARING UP?

NOT SO GOOD. IT'S SORT OF THE END OF AN ERA.

.."AND BEING OF ACCEPTABLY SOUND MIND AND WILL, I HEREBY LEAVE MY ENTIRE ESTATE TO.."

.."MY BELOVED PROTÉGÉ, MR. ZONKER HARRIS."

HUH?

OH, WOW..

YOU WERE HIS FAVORITE DEALER, I TAKE IT.

NO, NO, I'M AS SURPRISED AS YOU ARE!

YOU HEARD ME, PAL. PUT IT ALL IN ESCROW. NO ONE TOUCHES DUKE'S ESTATE UNTIL I SAY SO!

BUT, MR. HARRIS, WE'VE WORKED OUT A WHOLE INVESTMENT PROGRAM FOR YOU..

I'LL JUST BET YOU HAVE! WELL, YOU CAN FORGET IT! NOW, I HAVE A PLANE TO CATCH.

BE REASONABLE, MAN. WE COULD PUT YOUR MONEY TO WORK!

NO! AND THAT'S FINAL!

YOU'LL HAVE HIM DECLARED INSANE, OF COURSE.

CAN'T. THE JUDGE I USE IS ON VACATION.

GOOD EVENING. TODAY THE SMALL TOWN OF ROSEWATER, INDIANA, WAS HIT SUDDENLY BY A THREE-NETWORK MEDIA EVENT. IT WAS THE WORST MEDIA EVENT IN RECENT MEMORY.

THERE HAD BEEN NO WARNING. WHEN THE TINY LOCAL REPUBLICAN CAUCUS CONVENED LAST NIGHT FOR ITS PRESIDENTIAL STRAW POLL, ONLY LIGHT COVERAGE HAD BEEN FORECASTED..

BUT BEFORE IT WAS OVER, THE UNSUSPECTING TOWN WOULD BE BUFFETED BY WAVE AFTER WAVE OF REPORTERS, ITS CITIZENS INTERVIEWED AGAIN AND AGAIN, LEAVING THEM DAZED AND FAMOUS. ROLAND HEDLEY HAS DETAILS.

PEOPLE WERE JUST SITTING DOWN TO DINNER WHEN WALTER CRONKITE'S LIMOUSINE GLIDED UP TO RAY'S TACKLE SHOP..

THIS IS ROLAND HEDLEY. IT WAS SHORTLY AFTER DUSK WHEN THE MEDIA EVENT FIRST SWEPT THROUGH THE SMALL HOOSIER HAMLET OF ROSEWATER..

MEMBERS OF THE ROSEWATER G.O.P. CAUCUS HAD JUST CAST THE FIRST BALLOT IN A PRESIDENTIAL STRAW POLL. CAUCUS MEMBER AL FENDER EXPLAINS WHAT HAPPENED NEXT.

IT WAS AWFUL.. THE HOT LIGHTS, THE CAMERAS. SOME OF US TRIED TO STAY OFF THE RECORD, BUT IT WAS HOPELESS. WE WERE FORCED TO STAND BY HELPLESSLY AS OUR REMARKS WERE BLOWN ALL OUT OF PROPORTION!

AND THE POLL RESULTS?

STRIPPED OF THEIR CONTEXT! RIGHT THERE IN FRONT OF OUR FAMILIES!

A MEDIA EVENT. UNTIL LAST NIGHT, FOR THE PEOPLE OF ROSEWATER IT HAD ONLY BEEN AN EXPRESSION. VICTIMS RAY AND ELLEN McNEIL RECALL THEIR NIGHTMARE.

I GUESS IT STARTED RIGHT AFTER THE CAUCUS VOTE. THE FAMILY HAD PICKED ME UP AT THE VFW HALL, AND WE WALKED THE FEW BLOCKS HOME..

AS WE GOT TO THE FRONT YARD, I SEE THIS FELLER IN A SAFARI-TYPE JACKET RUNNING AT US. HE WAS YELLING AND WAVING AND KEPT TRIPPING OVER THIS LONG, PURPLE SCARF. IT WAS GERALDO RIVERA.

"GET THE KIDS INSIDE," I SHOUTED TO ELLEN..

WE WERE SCARED. WE'D SEEN WHAT HE'D DONE TO ELVIS'S DOCTOR.

FOR THE CITIZENS OF ROSEWATER, THE MEDIA EVENT IS OVER. BUT THE SCARS LINGER ON. CAUCUS MEMBER SHELLY SIMMS SHARES HER TRAUMA AND SHAME.

WELL, I WAS JUST LEAVING THE VFW HALL WHEN I FIRST SAW THEM. I TRIED TO FLEE, BUT THERE WERE TOO MANY OF THEM. A BIG ONE, WITH A MICROPHONE, CORNERED ME..

I TRIED TO RESIST, I TRIED TO TELL HIM IT WAS JUST A STRAW POLL, THAT IT DIDN'T MEAN ANYTHING, BUT HE..HE..

HE WHAT, MS. SIMMS?

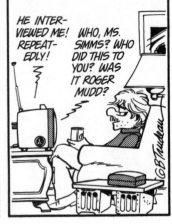

HE INTER-VIEWED ME! REPEAT-EDLY!

WHO, MS. SIMMS? WHO DID THIS TO YOU? WAS IT ROGER MUDD?

NOW THAT THE MEDIA CIRCUS HAS LEFT TOWN, THE VICTIMS OF THIS SENSE-LESS, MINDLESS COVERAGE MUST TRY TO PICK UP THE PIECES. HOMEMAKER DOTTY HOLMES TALKS OF HER DESPAIR.

IT'S HARDEST ON MY THREE KIDS. THEY'RE HEARTBROKEN. THEY KEEP ASKING ME, "MOMMY, WHEN ARE THE T.V. PEOPLE COMING BACK?"

I DON'T KNOW WHAT WE'LL DO. ABC NEWS PROMISED US THERE'D BE A FOLLOW-UP STORY, BUT WE DON'T HAVE MUCH HOPE THAT ANYTHING WILL COME OF IT..

THIS IS THE FOLLOW-UP STORY, MRS. HOLMES.

OH. WELL, IT'S JUST NOT THE SAME.

HELLO?

HELLO, MS. CAUCUS? THIS IS MS. HUAN, J.J.'S ROOM-MATE..

WHY, YES, HOW ARE YOU, DEAR?

FINE, THANKS. J.J. ASKED ME TO CALL YOU AND TELL YOU SHE JUST LEFT FOR YOUR PLACE..

SHE HAS TO MEET HER BOYFRIEND ZEKE AT THE AIRPORT, THOUGH, SO SHE'LL ONLY HAVE ABOUT TEN MINUTES FOR DINNER..

WELL, WE'LL CERTAINLY BE LOOKING FOR-WARD TO THAT, DEAR.

SHE DOESN'T WANT ANY-THING FANCY. JUST A LIGHT SALAD.

HI, RICK. LOOK, I HAVE TO MEET ZEKE AT THE AIRPORT, SO I CAN'T STAY FOR VERY LONG..

IT'S PROBABLY JUST AS WELL. MOM'S BEEN ON MY CASE A LOT LATELY, WHICH I'M NOT SURE SHE'S ENTI-TLED TO. YOU GUYS HAVEN'T BEEN FIGHTING, HAVE YOU?

LISTEN, WHEN I BRING ZEKE BY AFTER DINNER, TRY NOT TO BE TOO JUDGMENTAL, OKAY? HE'S A LIBRA AND VERY SENSITIVE.

HI, JOAN. WON'T YOU COME IN?

OH, MOM! YOU'RE NOT SERVING MEAT!

A FOOTNOTE'S PROGRESS

Q: You have been accused by numerous political observers of aiding and abetting the Anderson campaign. How do you plead?

A: Puzzlement. Anyone dumb enough to get his political information from a comic strip deserves what he gets at the polls. The Anderson strips were perceived as kindly, and thus an endorsement. The candidate's own view of the cartoon connection changed from week to week. At first he was disturbed, then he started quoting the strip in every speech. Later, both he and his campaign manager repudiated it.[1] It made it very hard for the public to keep abreast of the impact I was supposed to be having. In the end, I think I only swayed about three or four million votes, although which way I can't be sure.

[1]Anderson's final assessment: "I don't regard *Doonesbury* as the apotheosis of what the John Anderson campaign is all about."

WHAT'S ALL THIS, MIKE?

INVITES. FOR OUR "FIN DE DECADE" PARTY.

INVITES? LITTLE BOTTLES OF PERRIER?

READ THE LABEL.

"GET IT TOGETHER, GET IT ON, AND GET IT OVER WITH. YOU ARE INVITED TO A SEVENTIES REVIVAL. DRESS: DISCO/MELLOW."

A COME-AS-YOU-ARE PARTY?

RIGHT. WE'RE ASKING EVERYONE TO TAKE RESPONSIBILITY FOR HIS OWN COSTUME.

©B Trudeau

A SEVENTIES REVIVAL PARTY! I LIKE IT!

WELL, I THOUGHT WE SHOULD GET IT OVER WITH. BESIDES, IT'S RIFE WITH POSSIBILITIES!

IT SURE IS! I THINK I'LL COME AS A MOONIE.

YOU'LL NEVER GET IN.

I WON'T?

NOPE. WE'RE HIRING BOUNCERS. GUESTS WHO AREN'T FAMOUS WILL HAVE TO WAIT OUTSIDE IN THE COLD FOR 15 MINUTES.

I GUESS YOU HAVE TO DRAW THE LINE SOMEWHERE.

RIGHT. BESIDES, ANYONE WHO COULDN'T GET ON A TALK SHOW DURING THE '70s WASN'T TRYING.

©B Trudeau

WHO ARE YOU COMING TO THE PARTY AS, MIKE?

WELL, I WAS THINKING OF STEVE RUBELL, THE OWNER OF STUDIO 54.

VERY IMAGINATIVE. BUT DO YOU KNOW YOUR WAY AROUND A CELEBRITY?

I THINK SO. MY COUSIN'S A CELEBRITY. HE'S DAVE POPKIN.

WALDEN

WHO'S DAVE POPKIN?

ARE YOU KIDDING? HE'S ONE OF ONLY THREE PEOPLE IN ALL OF LOS ANGELES WHO HAVE NEVER BEEN PROFILED IN "PEOPLE"!

WOW.. THAT'S INCREDIBLE..

YOU BET IT IS. HE'S BEEN WRITTEN UP ALL OVER THE PLACE.

GB Trudeau

I CAN'T STAND IT. THAT BOZO'S ABOUT TO PUT ON ANOTHER DISCO RECORD!

COURAGE, OL' BUDDY. DISCO'S DAYS ARE NUMBERED.

THAT'S PRETTY PHILOSOPHICAL OF YOU, MICHAEL.

ONLY WAY I MADE IT THROUGH THE DECADE. I JUST KEPT REMEMBERING MY GRANDMA'S FAVORITE ADAGE, "THIS, TOO, WILL PASS."

AND YOUR GRANDMOTHER WAS RIGHT! THE SEVENTIES DID JUST THAT!

THEY DID, INDEED!

TO A KIDNEY STONE OF A DECADE!

TO THE WORST OF TIMES!

CLIK!

TOOT, TOOT! BEEP, BEEP!

GB Trudeau

MR. AFSHAR, COULD YOU COMMENT ON THE REPORT THAT SEVERAL OF YOUR FELLOW TERRORISTS ARE NO LONGER IN GOOD ACADEMIC STANDING?

THESE LIES ARE AS FOUL AND NOXIOUS AS THE SPUTUM OF A CAMEL. WE ARE ALL TRUE BELIEVERS, AND WE CAN ONLY FAIL IF ALLAH WILLS IT.

THE ACADEMIC PRESSURE THAT DOES EXIST IS QUITE NORMAL. NATURALLY, EACH OF US IS ANXIOUS TO TAKE HIS PLACE IN THE NEW ISLAMIC SOCIETY. WITH 40% UNEMPLOYMENT, SOME COMPETITION IS INEVITABLE.

ANY CHEATING?

VERY LITTLE. ONLY AMONG THE PREMEDS.

MR. AFSHAR, WHAT IS YOUR REACTION TO THE REPORT THAT STUDENTS WITH THE WORST ACADEMIC PROBLEMS HAVE BEEN ROTATED FROM DUTY?

THESE FALSEHOODS FESTER IN THE MOUTHS OF ZIONIST JACK-RABBITS. THE STUDENTS WHO LED THIS MOST HOLY ATTACK ARE STILL WITHIN THE COMPOUND.

WE HAVE REMAINED AT OUR POSTS THROUGHOUT, EVEN ON THE FIRST SATURDAY OF DECEMBER, WHICH IS, OF COURSE, SACRED TO US.

SACRED? HOW SO?

HOMECOMING. THE BIG SOCCER GAME WITH QOM TECH.

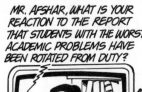

HEY, ZONKER, YOU GOT AN OVERNIGHT BAG?

UNDER MY BED. YOU GOING SOMEWHERE?

WELL, IF I CAN TALK MIKE OUT OF HIS CAR, I'D LIKE TO GO HOME TOMORROW. IS HE AROUND?

IN THE KITCHEN. HE'S WORKING ON A DATE FOR NEW YEAR'S.

STILL?

THESE THINGS TAKE TIME.

YES?

HI, YOU DON'T KNOW ME, BUT I SAW YOUR PICTURE IN THE STUDENT DIRECTORY, AND I..

TEN!.. NINE!..

EIGHT!.. SEVEN!.. SIX!..

FIVE!.. FOUR!.. THREE!..

HI, YOU DON'T KNOW ME, BUT..

OKAY, NOW, TRY NOT TO SOUND DESPERATE.

SENATOR KENNEDY, DO YOU AGREE WITH YOUR FELLOW CANDIDATES THAT THE PRESIDENT HAS MIS- HANDLED THE CRISIS IN AFGHANISTAN?

WELL, IN THIS MOMENT OF NATIONAL CRISIS, ANY SECOND-GUESSING THAT I.. ER.. PERSONALLY, WITH RE- SPECT TO THE INTERESTS OF PEACE.

MOREOVER, WITH THE.. UH.. UNCHALLENGED SOVIET THREAT, THE.. ER.. GRAIN EMBARGO WHICH.. UH.. AS FAR AS STRONG LEAD- ERSHIP IN THIS COUNTRY!

NOW, IN RESPECT TO THE..

A VERB, SENATOR, WE NEED A VERB!

GB Trudeau

GOVERNOR BROWN, DO YOU THINK PRESIDENT CARTER WAS RIGHT TO RULE OUT A MILITARY STRIKE TO FREE THE HOSTAGES IN TEHRAN?

ABSOLUTELY NOT. NO OPTION SHOULD EVER BE RULED OUT. ESPECIALLY IN THE FACE OF A SERIOUS THREAT TO THE VIABILITY OF STAR- SHIP AMERICA.

FOREIGN POLICY HAS TO BE VIEWED AS PROCESS. UNDER CERTAIN CIRCUM- STANCES, A MILITARY POSTURE SHOULD BE PER- MITTED TO EVOLVE.

WHAT SORT OF REACTION TIME ARE WE TALKING HERE, GOVERNOR?

WHATEVER FEELS RIGHT.

GB Trudeau

GENTLEMEN, ALL OF YOU HAVE BEEN EXTREMELY CRITICAL OF PRESIDENT CARTER'S ACTIONS, BUT NO ONE HAS SAID WHAT HE WOULD HAVE DONE DIFFERENTLY..

EACH OF YOU HAS IMPLIED THAT SOME SORT OF DIRECT MILITARY ACTION MIGHT HAVE BEEN IN ORDER. DOES ANYONE CARE TO GO ON THE RECORD AS ADVOCATING THAT? SENATOR BAKER?

MR. REDFERN, I'M AFRAID I CAN'T ANSWER THAT QUESTION. THIS TIME NEXT YEAR I EX- PECT TO BE PRESIDENT, AND I'D RATHER NOT TIP MY HAND TO THE SOVIETS.

SAME HERE.

ME, TOO.

THANKS.

SORRY. GOOD QUESTION, THOUGH.

GB Trudeau

HEY, MARCUS, GUESS WHAT I JUST HEARD ON THE RADIO! JOHN ANDERSON IS GIVING A MAJOR CAMPAIGN SPEECH ON CAMPUS TONIGHT!

I KNOW. MIKE JUST WENT IN TO SEE HIM.

HOW EXCITING! MAYBE WE SHOULD GO, TOO!

YOU LIKE ANDERSON?

UM.. I DON'T KNOW. WHO IS HE?

I'D LIKE TO THANK ALL OF YOU FOR TURNING OUT TONIGHT..

MONDAY NIGHTS ARE ALWAYS BAD, SIR. IT'S NOT YOUR FAULT.

GB Trudeau

WELL, I GUESS WE BETTER GET STARTED.. MR. ANDERSON, I'D LIKE TO APOLOGIZE FOR THE POOR TURN-OUT TONIGHT. MONDAY NIGHTS ARE *ALWAYS* BAD HERE.

ALSO, THERE'S A BIG BASKETBALL GAME WITH COLUMBIA TONIGHT. EVERYBODY, BUT EVERYBODY, GOES TO THE COLUMBIA GAME. IT'S CONSIDERED PRETTY DE RIGUEUR.

SO, REALLY, IT'S NO REFLECTION ON YOUR CAMPAIGN. IT'S JUST A SCHEDULING CONFLICT. THE STUDENTS ALL BOUGHT TICKETS TO THE GAME MONTHS AGO, SO WHAT COULD THEY DO?

I SEE. WELL, THANK YOU FOR EXPLAINING. ALSO, WE'RE IN THE MIDDLE OF AN ANNETTE FUNICELLO FILM FESTIVAL. IT'S JUST BAD TIMING.

INEXPLICABLY, WE STILL PAY TRIBUTE TO THE EXTORTIONIST DEMANDS OF OPEC. INSTEAD OF PERMITTING THEM THE PRIVILEGE, WE SHOULD BE WILLING TO TAX CONSUMPTION OF GAS IN THIS COUNTRY! WOW..

CONGRESSMAN ANDERSON, THAT'S ONE OF THE MORE AUDACIOUS PROPOSALS OF THE YEAR. AND YET, BECAUSE YOU ARE SO UNCOMMONLY WELL-SPOKEN, THE IDEA SEEMS TO MAKE A GREAT DEAL OF SENSE.

THANK YOU. YOU HAVE QUITE A GIFT, SIR.. WHAT DO YOU EXPECT TO DO WITH IT?

RUN FOR PRESIDENT. OH, RIGHT. SORRY. CARRY ON.

NOW MORE THAN EVER, WE MUST NOT PERMIT OURSELVES TO BE OVERCOME WITH A NEW MISSILE MADNESS, A MINDLESS RENEWAL OF UNRESTRICTED COMPETITION.

BEFORE IT IS TOO LATE, WE MUST MOVE TO RATIFY SALT. SALT IS NOT A UNILATERAL FAVOR WE ARE DOING THE SOVIET UNION; WE SHOULD NOT BE PENALIZING OURSELVES FOR SOVIET BEHAVIOR!

EXCUSE ME, CONGRESSMAN ANDERSON, BUT ARE YOU *SURE* YOU'RE A REPUBLICAN? YOU SURE DON'T *SOUND* LIKE A REPUBLICAN!

GREAT. HEY, BUT WHAT DO I KNOW? I'M A DEMOCRAT.

YES, IT WILL TAKE MORE THAN HORTATORY EXPRESSIONS ABOUT LEADERSHIP TO RESTORE OUR FLAGGING NATIONAL FORTUNES. THAT'S WHY I'M RUNNING AND THAT'S WHY I NEED YOUR SUPPORT!

BRAVO! YEAA! CLAP! CLAP! CLAP!

WE WANT *ANDERSON!* WE WANT *ANDERSON!* STOMP! STOMP!

THANK YOU. COULD YOU TELL ME HOW TO GET TO THE BUS STATION? SURE. DO YOU NEED A LIFT?

ZONK? HI, IT'S MIKE. LISTEN, I'M DOWN AT THE BUS STATION..

CONGRESSMAN ANDERSON MISSED HIS BUS, SO I'M GOING TO DRIVE HIM UP TO CONCORD.

CONCORD? THAT'S FIVE HOURS!

I KNOW, BUT HE'S A GOOD GUY, AND HE NEEDS THE LIFT. ALSO, HE SAID I COULD ADVANCE FOR HIM IF I WANTED TO.

ADVANCE FOR HIM? WHAT DOES HE MEAN BY ADVANCE?

CONGRESSMAN? WHAT DO YOU MEAN BY ADVANCE?

IN MY CASE, IT MEANS YOU GET OUT OF THE CAR FIRST.

SO WHAT'S MICHAEL GOING TO DO ABOUT HIS COURSES?

I DON'T KNOW. I GUESS IT DEPENDS ON HOW LONG JOHN ANDERSON CAN KEEP HIS CAMPAIGN ALIVE.

IT'S PRETTY EXCITING, THOUGH, ISN'T IT? OUR MIKE, ADVANCING FOR A MAJOR POLITICAL CANDIDATE!

NEVER HEARD OF HIM.

HE'S NEVER HEARD OF YOU, EITHER. JUST READ IT, OKAY?

ANDERSON? I'VE NEVER HEARD OF HIM. ARE YOU SURE HE'S ON THE NEW HAMPSHIRE BALLOT?

YES, MA'AM. IN FACT, HE'S SPEAKING TONIGHT AT THE YMCA AT SIX O'CLOCK.

SIX O'CLOCK? WELL, LET ME JUST CHECK MY BOOK.. LET'S SEE.. I'M SUPPOSED TO MEET BAKER OVER AT THE VFW HALL.. THAT'S AT FOUR..

AND CONNALLY'S DUE TO DROP BY THE PLANT RIGHT AFTER THAT.. AND, WELL, I PROMISED THE BUSH WORKERS WE'D MEET THEIR MAN OVER DINNER...IT DOESN'T LOOK GOOD..

BUT, HEY, IF ANYTHING SHOULD OPEN UP..

YOU PEOPLE ARE SPOILED ROTTEN, YOU KNOW THAT?

I'M SORRY, I'VE NEVER HEARD OF JOHN ANDERSON. BESIDES, I'M PRETTY APOLITICAL..

LOOK, JUST READ HIS FLIER, OKAY? WHAT DO YOU HAVE TO LOSE?

>SIGH<..OKAY, IF YOU INSIST.. HMM.. HMM.. ..UH-HUH..

HMM..THAT MAKES SENSE..HMM, I NEVER THOUGHT OF IT THAT WAY.. YES.. RIGHT..YES, YES, THAT'S SO TRUE! BOY, THAT'S TRUE!

MAN! I THINK I'LL QUIT MY JOB AND GO WORK FOR THIS GUY!

PRETTY PERSUASIVE, ISN'T HE?

CONGRESSMAN? THIS IS DANNY WATTLE. HE'D LIKE TO SIGN UP FOR THE CAMPAIGN!

I REALLY LIKED YOUR FLIER, SIR. DID YOU WRITE IT YOURSELF?

UH..YES, I DID.

GREAT STUFF. THE LAYOUT WAS NICE, TOO. VERY EFFECTIVE GRAPHICS.

DO YOU THINK YOU COULD GIVE DAN YOUR CAMPAIGN SPEECH, SIR? I THINK HE'D ENJOY HEARING IT!

SPEECH? YOU'VE GOT A SPEECH, TOO?

WELL, I SUPPOSE I COULD SAY A FEW..

IT'S REALLY GOOD. I'VE HEARD IT.

BOY, IS THIS GREAT!

THANK YOU VERY MUCH FOR YOUR ATTENTION..

BRAVO! GREAT SPEECH! JUST SUPERB, SIR!

CLAP! CLAP!

I'M GOING TO HAVE TO CALL MY BROTHER-IN-LAW IN LACONIA. HE'S PRETTY APOLITICAL, TOO, BUT WHEN HE HEARS WHAT YOU HAVE TO SAY, I THINK HE'LL CHANGE HIS TUNE PDQ!

THEN, IF HE AND I BOTH TELL TWO MORE PEOPLE, AND THEN **THEY** TELL TWO PEOPLE EACH, ETC., WHY, THE PYRAMIDING EFFECT COULD PUT YOU IN BUSINESS!

I THINK WE'VE GOT SOMETHING OF A GROUNDSWELL ON OUR HANDS, SIR.

I'M GOING TO GET ON THE HORN RIGHT NOW!

GOOD EVENING. TODAY THE FIRST MAJOR SCANDAL OF THE '80'S SWEPT THROUGH THE NATION'S CAPITAL LIKE A TIDAL WAVE. ROLAND HEDLEY WAS THERE.

THE NEWS HIT WASHINGTON LIKE A BOMBSHELL. CONGRESSIONAL INVESTIGATORS HAD LINKED ATTORNEY GENERAL BENJAMIN CIVILETTI TO THE LARGEST ENTRAPMENT SCANDAL IN U.S. HISTORY.

ALSO CHARGED THIS MORNING WERE FBI DIRECTOR WILLIAM WEBSTER AND SEVERAL FEDERAL AGENTS WHO ALLEGEDLY RAN THE ENTRAPMENT RING OUT OF A POSH WASHINGTON TOWN HOUSE.

A TEAM OF SEVEN CONGRESSMEN, WORKING WITH A U.S. SENATOR, IS SAID TO HAVE BROKEN THE RING.

THEY'RE CALLING IT "CONSCAM." SEVERAL CONGRESSMEN, POSING AS THEMSELVES, HAVE BROKEN WHAT IS THOUGHT TO BE THE LARGEST ENTRAPMENT RING IN FBI HISTORY.

IT ALL TOOK PLACE IN THIS EXPENSIVE BRICK WASHINGTON COLONIAL. IT WAS HERE THAT FBI AGENTS REPEATEDLY URGED LEGISLATORS TO BREAK THE LAW AGAINST THEIR WILL.

THE FULL SCOPE OF THE RING'S ACTIVITIES IS STILL UNKNOWN, BUT THE D.C. OPERATION IS THOUGHT TO BE ONLY PART OF A MASSIVE, NATIONWIDE SCHEME TO DISCREDIT AND SMEAR PROMINENT PUBLIC OFFICIALS.

FBI MOTIVES WERE UNCERTAIN. BACK AFTER THIS.

HOW DID THE LEGISLATORS GATHER ENOUGH EVIDENCE TO BUST UP THE FBI ENTRAPMENT RING? I ASKED ONE OF THE CONGRESSMEN INVOLVED..

PIECE OF CAKE, REALLY. I SIMPLY PUT OUT THE WORD I WAS OPEN TO A BRIBE. THE RUSE WORKED LIKE A CHARM. WITHIN DAYS, I WAS BEING HANDED $50,000 IN TAXPAYERS' MONEY!

IN THE WEEKS THAT FOLLOWED, THE SCOPE OF MY INVESTIGATION WIDENED. TO MY SHOCK, I WAS OFFERED BRIBES BY AGENTS IN NEW JERSEY, NEW YORK, FLORIDA, EVEN TEXAS!

CONGRESSMAN, DID YOU FIND ANY HONEST FBI AGENTS?

ONLY ONE. BUT HE WAS GREAT. HE WOULDN'T GIVE ME A DIME.

IF THIS SCANDAL HAS A HERO, THEN SURELY IT IS ARMSTRONG ALGER, THE ONLY FBI AGENT TO REFUSE TO ENTRAP AN UNDERCOVER CONGRESSMAN. ALGER DESCRIBED THE ENCOUNTER TO ABC NEWS.

ACTUALLY IT WAS VERY BRIEF. HE SIMPLY TURNED UP AT THE HOUSE ONE NIGHT, SAID HE HAD HEARD ABOUT THE BRIBES AND WANTED A PIECE OF THE ACTION.

I REPLIED IT WAS UNETHICAL FOR ME TO ENTICE HIM INTO COMMITTING A CRIME HE WOULDN'T NORMALLY CONSIDER. THEN HE BECAME MAD AND STOMPED OUT OF THE HOUSE.

SO YOU DIDN'T GIVE HIM ANY MONEY AT ALL?

HE JUST WASN'T PREDISPOSED ENOUGH. LATER, HE CALLED TO CONGRATULATE ME.

WHAT WAS IT LIKE LIVING NEXT DOOR TO AN FBI ENTRAPMENT RING? NEIGHBOR WILBER FILBIS TALKED TO ABC WIDE WORLD OF NEWS ABOUT HIS ORDEAL...

LISTEN, I GOT THREE KIDS. IT'S HARD ENOUGH KEEPING THEM AWAY FROM PUSHERS AT THE PLAYGROUND WITHOUT HAVING TO WORRY ABOUT WHITE COLLAR CRIME NEXT DOOR!

IT'S SORT OF CREEPY, Y'KNOW? JUST KNOWING THAT RIGHT ACROSS THE STREET, PEOPLE WERE BEING INDUCED TO COMMIT CRIMES WITHOUT ANY PREDISPOSITION AT ALL!

EVER HEAR ANY SCREAMS?

NO, BUT WE KNEW THEY WERE BAD NEWS. THEY ALL CARRIED GUNS AND NEVER CAME TO BLOCK PARTIES.

G B Trudeau

FOR THE SPECIAL TEAM OF INVESTIGATING CONGRESSMEN, OPERATION "CONSCAM" IS OVER. ITS MISSION HAS BEEN COMPLETED.

BUT FOR ATTORNEY GENERAL BENJAMIN CIVILETTI AND THE SCORES OF FBI OFFICIALS IMPLICATED IN THE ENTRAPMENT SCANDAL, THE NIGHTMARE HAS JUST BEGUN.

TODAY AS HEARINGS GOT UNDER WAY, CONGRESSMEN CAME FORWARD ONE BY ONE TO TELL HORROR STORIES OF BEING WANTONLY HOUNDED INTO ACCEPTING MONEY THEY WANTED NO PART OF.

COUNTER-CHARGES THAT THEY TOOK THE BRIBES WILLINGLY ARE BEING LAUGHED OFF. THIS IS ROLAND HEDLEY.

COMING UP, TANNING ACE ZONKER HARRIS..

..WITH A FULL REPORT ON THE FORT LAUDERDALE SUN SPRINTS!

TODAY ON "PROFILES ON PARADE," WE'RE DELIGHTED TO WELCOME TANNING EXPERT ZONKER HARRIS. ZONKER, I UNDERSTAND YOU'RE JUST BACK FROM THE FORT LAUDERDALE SUN SPRINTS.

THAT'S RIGHT, MARK, I WAS THERE COMPETING ON A COPPERTONE FELLOWSHIP. AS PART OF THE PROGRAM, I'LL ALSO BE TRAVELING TO CALIFORNIA THIS SUMMER, TO STUDY UNDER THE GREAT TANMASTER GEORGE HAMILTON AT HIS WORKSHOP IN MALIBU.

THAT'S QUITE AN HONOR. HOW DO YOU GET SELECTED FOR A FELLOWSHIP?

WELL, YOU HAVE TO SUBMIT A PORTFOLIO OF COLOR SLIDES, ALONG WITH AFFIDAVITS FROM YOUR DERMATOLOGIST.

DO YOU REGARD THIS AS A CAREER MOVE? WHAT SORT OF PROSPECTS DO YOU FACE AS A TRAINED TANNIST?

WELL, MARK, THERE IS A GROWING NUMBER OF OPPORTUNITIES IN THE AREA OF SHOW TANNING, BUT FULL-TIME EMPLOYMENT IS STILL PRETTY SCARCE.

IN FACT, GEORGE HIMSELF IS PROBABLY THE ONLY PERSON TO EVER PARLAY A TAN INTO A WHOLE CAREER, ALTHOUGH HE **HAS** PLACED SEVERAL GRADUATES FROM HIS CLINIC ON "HOLLYWOOD SQUARES."

THAT'S THE ONLY SHOW WHICH TAKES TAN PEOPLE?

WELL, IT'S THE ONLY ONE WHICH ACTUALLY **PAYS** YOU TO BE TAN.

GB Trudeau

YOU REALLY WROTE A BOOK, ZEKE? I DIDN'T KNOW YOU WERE A WRITER.

I DIDN'T EITHER, MAN. IT WAS SORT OF AN UNTAPPED TALENT.

AND NOW HE'S ON THE WAY TO FAME AND FORTUNE!

THERE'S GOING TO BE A WHOLE BOOK TOUR, MOTHER. ZEKE'S GOING TO DO TALK SHOWS, BOOK SIGNINGS, INTERVIEWS, THE WORKS!

YOU MUST BE VERY EXCITED, ZEKE.

YEAH, I AM, MAN. I JUST HOPE I DON'T OUTGROW MY FAMILY AND FRIENDS.

IT'S GOT US BOTH WORRIED. ZEKE KNOWS PEOPLE THAT'S HAPPENED TO.

I THINK THE BOOK CALLS FOR A SMALL CELEBRATION, DON'T YOU, DEAR?

CHAMPAGNE? GEE, THAT'S GREAT OF YOU, MOM.

WHERE'D ZEKE GO?

OH, HE WENT UPSTAIRS TO BREAK THE NEWS TO RICK.

WHAT DO YOU MEAN, BREAK THE NEWS?

WELL, SINCE RICK IS A WRITER, TOO, ZEKE'S WORRIED HE'LL BE A LITTLE JEALOUS.

HOW'S THAT?

$100,000. YOU'RE NOT JEALOUS, ARE YOU, MAN?

SO YOU THINK YOU'LL BE HITTING THE TALK SHOW CIRCUIT, ZEKE?

OH, FOR SURE, MAN. HELL, THAT'S THE BEST PART OF PUBLISHING A BOOK!

THE ACTUAL AUTHORING, THOUGH, IS SOMETHING ELSE. WRITING A BOOK REQUIRES PATIENCE, CONCENTRATION AND AN INCREDIBLE AMOUNT OF SELF-DISCIPLINE.

WOW..

SO WHAT'D YOU DO, HIRE A GHOST?

RICK! OF COURSE NOT!

MORE LIKE A PROOFREADER, REALLY.

GOOD MORNING. ANDERSON FOR PRESIDENT.

YEAH, THIS IS CURT WILKIE FROM THE "GLOBE.."

YES, MR. WILKIE. MAY I HELP YOU?

YEAH, I'M TRYING TO WRAP UP HERE, AND I WAS WONDERING IF THE CANDIDATE HAD ANY LAST-MINUTE PLATITUDES BEFORE TODAY'S PRIMARY.

I'M AFRAID NOT, SIR. MR. ANDERSON ONLY TALKS IN SPECIFICS. BUT I COULD GET YOU AN EPIGRAM IF YOU WANT.

EPIGRAM? WHAT AM I GOING TO DO WITH AN EPIGRAM? I WAS TOLD HE'D HAVE A PLATITUDE.

I'M SORRY, SIR. THIS IS A CAMPAIGN OF IDEAS.

"THIS IS A CAMPAIGN OF IDEAS," OKAY, THAT'S GOOD ENOUGH.

MUFFY, I SWEAR, YOU LOOK JUST AS GOOD AS WHEN I FIRST SAW YOU ON THE DANCE FLOOR TWENTY YEARS AGO.

THAT WAS QUITE A SUMMER, WASN'T IT, SAMMY?

I STILL THINK ABOUT IT. REMEMBER OUR CHANCE MEETING BEHIND THE STABLES OUT AT THE CLUB?..

SAM, FOR GOD'S SAKE, NOT WITH THE BARTENDER LISTENING..

OH, NEVER MIND HIM. HE'S HEARD IT ALL BEFORE, HAVEN'T YOU, BARTENDER?

YES, SIR, I SUPPOSE I HAVE.

YEAH, I TOOK ONE LOOK AT YOUR RIDING CROP, AND..

GO.

I'M OUT OF HERE.

BOY, EDDIE, WE SURE HAD SOME TIMES TOGETHER, DIDN'T WE? REMEMBER TAKING HISTORY FROM OL' MAN GOLDFARB? BOY, DID WE GIVE HIM A HARD TIME, REMEMBER?

LIKE THE TIME WE RAN THAT PICTURE OF HIM AND THAT COED IN THE SCHOOL PAPER. REMEMBER WHAT HAPPENED THEN?

YES. HIS WIFE LEFT HIM AND HE RESIGNED IN DISGRACE.

OH.. THAT'S RIGHT..

I COULDA SWORN THAT STORY HAD A FUNNY ENDING.

HE DIED, TOO, BUT I GUESS THAT WASN'T OUR FAULT.

YOU'RE STILL NOT MARRIED EITHER? AN ATTRACTIVE WOMAN LIKE YOU, CATHY?

OH, HARRY, HARRY, MAYBE YOU WERE THE ONE, AFTER ALL.

BUT I'M IN OIL NOW, CATHY. HOW COULD YOU EVER RESPECT SOMEONE LIKE ME?

WHAT DIFFERENCE COULD THAT MAKE, HARRY?

BARTENDER, WHAT DO YOU AND YOUR FRIENDS THINK OF PEOPLE IN THE OIL INDUSTRY?

WE THINK THEY'RE A BUNCH OF CONTEMPTIBLE GREEDHEADS.

SEE? OUR CHILDREN WOULD LIVE WITH THAT EVERY DAY..

WE COULD HIRE TUTORS. OH, DARLING, TOGETHER WE COULD MAKE A STAND!

ONLY A FEW QUESTIONS, LADIES AND GENTLEMEN. THE GOVERNOR IS ANXIOUS TO GET ON WITH THE REST OF HIS NONSTOP 18-HOUR DAY OF CAMPAIGNING.

GOVERNOR REAGAN, LATELY YOU'VE BEEN CHARACTERIZED IN THE PRESS AS A WALKING ENCYCLOPEDIA OF INACCURATE STORIES AND DATED, HEARSAY STATISTICS. ANY COMMENT?

WELL, TO BEGIN WITH, THAT'S A CURIOUS ACCUSATION COMING FROM THE PRESS, SINCE LIKE 95% OF ALL AMERICANS, I GET MOST OF MY INFORMATION FROM NEWSPAPERS.

ACTUALLY, SIR, THAT FIGURE IS CLOSER TO 45%.

LET'S CALL IT AN EVEN 70.

THAT SEEMS FAIR.

..AND WHILE IT'S TRUE THAT SOME OF MY CLIPPINGS FROM "LIBERTY" AND "COLLIER'S" ARE A BIT DATED, MOST OF THEM HAVE AS MUCH SIGNIFICANCE FOR US NOW AS THEY DID IN THE '30'S.

FOR EXAMPLE, DID YOU KNOW THIS? "STUDIES NOW SHOW THAT NEARLY 95% OF ALL PEOPLE ON THE PUBLIC DOLE ROUTINELY TURN DOWN HONEST WORK WHEN IT IS OFFERED TO THEM."

THAT'S VERY INTERESTING, GOVERNOR. YOU REALIZE, OF COURSE, THAT THAT'S UTTERLY PREPOSTEROUS.

I ONLY KNOW WHAT I READ.

YES, SIR. I THINK THAT'S WHAT'S GOT EVERYONE SO CONCERNED.

UM..OKAY, YOU GUYS ALL KNOW ME. I'M BROOKS HARKNESS, PRESIDENT OF THE SIXTH FORM..

TODAY WE AT ST. GROTTLESEX PREP ARE PRIVILEGED TO WELCOME PRESIDENTIAL CANDIDATE GEORGE BUSH, ANDOVER '42, AND YALE '48!

AMBASSADOR BUSH, IF I MAY, I'D LIKE TO ASK THE FIRST QUESTION..

FABULOUS! LET'S GET A DIALOGUE GOING HERE!

WHAT WOULD YOU DO TO MAKE GOVERNMENT LESS TACKY?

I'D DO LOADS! THIS IS A GREAT COUNTRY! GOVERNMENT DOESN'T HAVE TO BE TACKY!

AMBASSADOR BUSH, HAS BEING A PREPPIE HURT YOUR CAREER?

ON THE CONTRARY! I'VE FOUND THAT WHEN GIVEN A CHOICE, PEOPLE ACTUALLY PREFER TO VOTE PREPPIE!

AND WHY NOT? WE'VE GOT THE TRACK RECORD! WHY, OUR GREAT BOARDING SCHOOLS AND IVY LEAGUE COLLEGES HAVE ALWAYS PRODUCED MORE THAN THEIR FAIR SHARE OF LEADERS!

THINK ABOUT IT! WHAT DID SUCH GREAT PRESIDENTS AS WOODROW WILSON, FRANKLIN ROOSEVELT AND JOHN KENNEDY ALL HAVE IN — COMMON?

THEY ALL GOT US INTO WAR?

RIGHT! THESE SCHOOLS JUST DON'T TURN OUT SISSIES!

AMBASSADOR BUSH, DO YOU FAVOR FEDERAL GUARANTEES ON SUMMER VACATION LOANS?

GOSH, YES!

I THINK WE HAVE A SERIOUS YOUTH PROBLEM IN THIS COUNTRY! ANY TIME YOU HAVE TOO MANY KIDS LANGUISHING AT OUR BADLY CONGESTED COUNTRY CLUBS, YOU HAVE AN EXPLOSIVE SITUATION!

I THINK EVERY YOUNG MAN OR WOMEN OVER 16 SHOULD BE REQUIRED TO SPEND AT LEAST TWO MONTHS SUMMERING IN EUROPE. I WOULD FAVOR THAT KIND OF PROGRAM.

WHAT IF THEY REFUSED TO GO?

I'D USE FORCE. AFTER CONSULTING WITH THE AFFECTED NATIONS, OF COURSE.

THE GERALD R. FORD PRO-AM SUMMER BI-ATHLON? WHAT IS A SUMMER BIATHLON, Z.?

IT'S A COMBINA-TION GOLF AND TAN-NING EVENT.

IT'S ONE OF THE MOST PRESTIGIOUS EVENTS OF ITS KIND. USUALLY, ONLY TOP LEISURE SPECIALISTS LIKE BRUCE JENNER ARE INVITED TO PARTICIPATE.

IN PAST YEARS, SOME OF THE TRULY LEGENDARY TANS HAVE BEEN SHOWCASED AT THE FORD BIATHLON—THE '67 SINATRA TAN, THE '73 CHER TAN, THE '77 ANDY WILLIAMS TAN..

YOU MEAN TANNISTS HAVE GOOD AND BAD YEARS?

SURE. EVEN THE BEST. HELL, GEORGE HAMIL-TON'S '63 TAN WAS A **HUGE** SCANDAL.

TELL ME, ZONK, HOW DID OUR FORMER PRESIDENT GET INTERESTED IN THE SUMMER BIATHLON IN THE FIRST PLACE?

WELL, ACCORDING TO THE TOURNAMENT PROGRAM, IT WAS ALL THE RESULT OF A RATHER HAPPY ACCIDENT..

MR. FORD WAS OUT ON THE LINKS ONE DAY WHEN HIS GOLF CART BROKE DOWN. HE DECIDED TO HOOF IT. AT THE END OF THE DAY, HE FOUND THAT NOT ONLY HAD HE SHOT 18 HOLES OF GOLF, BUT HE'D ALSO ACQUIRED A ROSY TAN!

AT THE SAME TIME?

IT WAS SOMETHING OF A BREAK-THROUGH.

I THOUGHT YOU HAD TO TRAIN TODAY, ZONK.

I DO, BUT FIRST I HAVE TO DECIDE WHICH TAN TO GO WITH.

I'VE BEEN GOING THROUGH THE "COPPERTONE GUIDE TO GREAT TANS OF THE SOUTHWEST." SO FAR, I'VE GOT THEM NARROWED DOWN TO "GAUCHO GLOW" AND "ALAMO SUNSET."

"GAUCHO GLOW" IS DESCRIBED AS "ROBUST, FULL-BODIED, A MAN'S TAN, DEEP AND EXCITING." "ALAMO SUNSET" IS "UNPRETENTIOUS BUT TART, AN AMUSING LITTLE COUNTRY TAN."

AN AMUSING LITTLE COUN-TRY TAN?

DON'T LAUGH. IT SWEPT THE GOLD AND SIL-VER AT PHOENIX LAST YEAR.

MIKE, IF ANYONE CALLS, I'LL BE OUT BEHIND THE BARN WORKING ON MY SLICE AND TAN.

OKAY. WHICH TAN DID YOU DECIDE TO SHOOT FOR?

I SETTLED ON A NUMBER CALLED "FREEWAY BOLD." SONNY BONO SPORTED IT DURING HIS UPSET WIN AT THE '79 CHERYL TIEGS DESERT CLASSIC..

THE LITERATURE DESCRIBES IT AS "A FLASHY TROPICAL TAN, A PRE-CANCEROUS GLOW FAVORED BY THE PROS."

SOUNDS PROMISING.

YOU BET IT DOES. TAKE A LOOK AT THESE COL-OR SWATCHES.

HMM.. NOT BAD. BUT DON'T THEY ALWAYS TOUCH THEM UP IN THE BROCHURE?

I REALLY SHOULDN'T BE DRIVING YOU INTO TEHRAN WITHOUT A WORK ORDER FROM THE IMAM. I COULD GET MY HANDS CHOPPED OFF.

WELL, I APPRECIATE YOUR ACCEPTING A BRIBE. I REALLY DO.

IT'S BEEN A WHILE. WE DON'T GET TOO MANY WESTERNERS IN TOWN ANYMORE.

THE ONLY AMERICANS WE'VE SEEN IN MONTHS ARE THE LIARS AND DEMONS OF THE U.S. PRESS. YOU HAIL FROM THE GREAT SATAN YOURSELF, RIGHT?

UH.. RIGHT. NEW YORK, ACTUALLY.

I CAN ALWAYS TELL. HOW LONG YOU BEEN WORKING FOR THE CIA?

ANY SIGN OF THE REV ON THE NEWS, MIKE?

NOT SO FAR.

I GUESS HE HASN'T GOTTEN IN TO SEE THE HOSTAGES YET.

WELL, THAT'S NOT SURPRISING..

HE'S UNDOUBTEDLY GOT A LOT OF HIGH LEVEL NEGOTIATIONS TO GET THROUGH FIRST.

HELLO? OPERATOR? I'M TRYING TO GET ROOM SERVICE.

SORRY, SIR. EVERYONE'S OUT FIGHTING THE LEFTISTS TODAY.

YES?

REVEREND SLOAN, I'M DR. ALI MAHDAVI, I'M FROM THE REVOLUTIONARY COUNCIL.

AT LAST! I WAS BEGINNING TO THINK I'D BEEN FORGOTTEN.

NOT AT ALL. MAY I COME IN?

WHY, OF COURSE, DR. MAHDAVI! PLEASE!

I CAN'T STAY LONG. I LEFT MY MOB OUTSIDE.

DEATH TO CARTER! DEATH TO CARTER!

YOU.. UH.. HAVE YOUR OWN MOB?

YES. WE'RE ON OUR WAY TO A FUNERAL.

REVEREND SLOAN, I CAN PERSONALLY ASSURE YOU THAT THE HOSTAGES ARE STILL IN PERFECT PHYSICAL AND MENTAL HEALTH.

BUT AS A MAN OF GOD, YOU SHOULD BE AWARE OF THE STATE OF MORAL TURPITUDE WHICH EXISTS AMONG YOUR COUNTRYMEN..

JUST THIS MORNING, THE STUDENTS CONFISCATED THIS SMUT MAGAZINE FROM ONE OF THE HOSTAGES. LOOK HOW FAR THESE HEATHEN HAVE FALLEN!

GOOD LORD. THESE WOMEN ARE WEARING ..DRESSES!

MANY OF THEM IN BRIGHT COLORS. WE HAVE PROOF THIS MAGAZINE IS PRINTED BY THE CIA.

BUT YOU STILL HAVEN'T SAID WHEN I CAN SEE THE HOSTAGES, DR. MAHDAVI.

ALL IN GOOD TIME, FATHER, ALL IN GOOD TIME.

PERHAPS IF I COULD SPEAK TO SOMEONE IN AUTHORITY..

AUTHORITY? MY DEAR REVEREND, I AM THE AUTHORITY!

THE STUDENTS HAVE BEEN TOLD BY THE IMAM HIMSELF THEY ARE TO ANSWER TO ME! THE WELL-BEING OF THE HOSTAGES IS COMPLETELY IN MY HANDS!

GREAT. ANY IDEA WHERE THEY ARE?

I'M WORKING ON IT. LOOK, WHY DON'T YOU TAKE IN SOME OF THE SIGHTS?

HELLO?

REVEREND SLOAN? THIS IS PRESIDENT BANI SADR.

MR. PRESIDENT! BOY, AM I GLAD TO HEAR FROM YOU, SIR. WHEN AM I GOING TO GET TO SEE THE HOSTAGES?

ANY DAY NOW, REVEREND. AS SOON AS WE CAN MAKE ARRANGEMENTS..

I'D RUN YOU OVER TO SEE THEM MYSELF, BUT IT LOOKS LIKE I'M GOING TO BE TIED UP ALL WEEK.

DOING WHAT, SIR?

CLINGING TO POWER. BUT MONDAY FOR SURE, OKAY?

STILL NO WORD FROM THE REV. I HOPE HE'S OKAY..

I'M SURE HE'S FINE, MIKE. SAY, YOU GOT THE TIME?

SURE. IT'S ABOUT TEN AFTER ONE.

OH, NO.. I PROMISED MARK I'D CATCH HIS SHOW.

OH? WHO'S HE GOT ON?

FAMED SEXUAL ADVENTURER GAY TALESE. HE'S GOING TO BE READING FROM HIS LATEST MONOGRAPH.

"TALESE SMILED AND REACHED INTO HIS BLACK LEATHERETTE DOCTOR'S BAG.."

DON'T TOUCH THAT DIAL, BOYS AND GIRLS! MORE AFTER THIS..

OVER THE YEARS, WE'VE HAD HIGH PROFILES AND WE'VE HAD LOW PROFILES, BUT FEW SILHOUETTES HAVE LINGERED SO LONG ON THE CULTURAL LANDSCAPE AS THAT OF SEXUAL EXPLORATEUR GAY TALESE.

MR. TALESE IS JUST BACK FROM A NINE-YEAR SAFARI THROUGH THE PORN SHOPS AND MASSAGE PARLORS OF AMERICA, AND HE HAS PUT HIS FINDINGS IN HIS NEW BOOK, "THY NEIGHBOR'S WIFE." MR. TALESE, WHAT'S THE BOOK ABOUT?

WELL, BY WAY OF ANSWERING, IF I MAY, I'D LIKE TO READ SELECTED PASSAGES FROM THE BOOK ITSELF.

WE WERE HOPING YOU'D SAY THAT, MR. TALESE. TAKE IT AWAY.

"IN THE BEGINNING, GAY TALESE DIDN'T EVEN OWN A RAINCOAT.."

YOU'RE KIDDING!

"AS TALESE EMERGED FROM HIS '57 TRIUMPH, HIS EYES LOOKED UP HUNGRILY AT THE FLICKERING RED NEON SIGN THAT READ 'LIVE NUDE COEDS'.."

"HE BOUNDED UP THE THREE FLIGHTS OF STEPS, ANXIOUS TO KEEP HIS APPOINTMENT WITH THE VOLUPTUOUS CHEMISTRY MAJOR WHOSE PHOTO HE HAD SELECTED WITH SUCH CARE FROM THE MASSAGE PARLOR PICTURE BOOK."

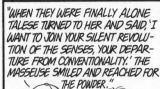

"WHEN THEY WERE FINALLY ALONE TALESE TURNED TO HER AND SAID, 'I WANT TO JOIN YOUR SILENT REVOLUTION OF THE SENSES, YOUR DEPARTURE FROM CONVENTIONALITY.' THE MASSEUSE SMILED AND REACHED FOR THE POWDER."

"MEANWHILE, OUT IN THE CAR, TALESE'S WIFE WAS GROWING IMPATIENT.."

UNDER-STANDABLY!

"IT WAS CLEAR TO TALESE THAT THE MASSAGE PARLOR WAS ON THE CUTTING EDGE OF THE NEW REVOLUTION.."

BUT YOU STILL HAVEN'T TOLD US WHAT THE BOOK'S ABOUT, MR. TALESE..

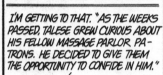

I'M GETTING TO THAT. "AS THE WEEKS PASSED, TALESE GREW CURIOUS ABOUT HIS FELLOW MASSAGE PARLOR PATRONS. HE DECIDED TO GIVE THEM THE OPPORTUNITY TO CONFIDE IN HIM."

"AFTER MONTHS OF SKILLFUL AND SENSITIVE INTERVIEWS, ONE OF THE CUSTOMERS FINALLY REVEALED THAT HE WAS MIDDLE-CLASS AND MARRIED. DAYS LATER, ANOTHER JOHN CONFESSED THAT HE, TOO, WAS MIDDLE-CLASS AND MARRIED."

"TALESE KNEW A TREND WHEN HE SAW ONE."

WOW.. I GUESS THAT'S THE ADVANTAGE OF BEING A REPORTER.

"NOTHING TALESE HAD EVER SEEN PREPARED HIM FOR THE EXPERIMENTS IN OPEN SEXUALITY HE WAS TO WITNESS THAT NIGHT AT THE SANDSTONE RETREAT.."

"ONLY A FEW FEET AWAY, SEXUAL PIONEERS WERE BREAKING NEW GROUND, PUSHING THE BOUNDARIES OF HONEST, OPEN COMMUNICATION BEYOND THE OUTER REACHES OF ACCEPTED SOCIAL BEHAVIOR."

"TALESE WENT UPSTAIRS WITH THREE OF HIS FELLOW REVOLUTIONARIES, AND FOR THE NEXT SEVERAL HOURS FLOUTED CONVENTION. SO PREOCCUPIED DID HE BECOME WITH HIS SILENT PROTEST AGAINST THE CENSORS AND CLERICS, HE FAILED TO HEAR A KNOCK."

"TALESE LOOKED UP TO SEE FOUR MORE PIONEERS."

HARDY STOCK, I HOPE.

HELLO?

REVEREND SLOAN? IT'S PRESIDENT BANI SADR.

YES, MR. PRESIDENT.

WE HAVE LOCATED THE HOSTAGES. DR. MAHDAVI WILL BE BY SHORTLY TO TAKE YOU TO THEM.

HELLO, REVEREND? DON'T LISTEN TO HIM! HE CAN'T DELIVER!

HEY! WHO'S THAT? IS THAT YOU, BEHESHTI?

HE DOESN'T HAVE THE AYATOLLAH'S EAR!

I DO, TOO! GET OFF THE LINE, YOU INSECT!